WOODSTOCK BEFORE WOODSTOCK

and

A BRIEF MILITARY HISTORY

I owe my success as a writer, in no small part, to the fact that I am in possession of an extraordinary memory. I can recall the smallest details of long ago events... whether they happened or not.

Mark Twain

I want to thank John Mower, Rod McLeod and all those who helped me to remember.

This book is for Aiden and Kiernan who caused me to remember in the first place.

WOODSTOCK
BEFORE
WOODSTOCK

FIRST MEMORY

Poking a stick into hot tar bubbles on the Saugerties road is just
about the first thing in my life that I recall. It is said that children
begin to form complete and permanent memories in the third or
fourth year of life. If we assume that to be an accurate estimate
then this first memory of mine must have formed in the summer of
1952.

My grandmother Elfleda was interested in piecing together
some of our family history. Toward that end she wanted very much
to visit a small graveyard on the south side of the route 212
between Woodstock and Saugerties.

It was not the custom for women of my grandmother's
generation to drive automobiles and she did not. She did, however,
spread the word among her friends who had cars that if anybody
was going to Saugerties they should give her a call.

In those days trips from Woodstock to Saugerties were as
common as trips to Kingston and among farm families even more
common. To understand this, one has to imagine what it was like

in the days before the automobile replaced the horse and wagon. While Saugerties and Kingston are roughly equidistant from Woodstock there are fewer hills on the Saugerties run and that can make a big difference to horses pulling loaded wagons. Commercial ties, formed in the horse and wagon days, lasted on into the automobile age. Only when route 28 was widened and the dip down into Stony Hollow eliminated did these bonds between Saugerties and the farm families of the Woodstock Valley begin to disintegrate.

For some reason I was spending the day with my grandmother when the phone call she had been waiting for finally came. We ate an early lunch and walked to the end of the lane to await our ride. In short order I found myself sitting in the back of a large, dusty, pre-war automobile. The car had been parked in the sun. I remember the warm smell of the cracked leather seat.

Fleda sat in the front and talked with the driver, a woman whose name is lost to me now. In fact, I don't recall anything about this other lady except for a small, black hat she wore. The hat was decorated with a bit of a veil turned up along the brim. It was, no doubt, a souvenir of her widowhood.

In time my grandmother pointed out the graveyard and the car braked to a stop on the east side of a small bridge. We got out and

Fleda leaned back into the car and went over the pick-up arrangements one last time with the driver.

"We'll be right here waiting for you on your way back," my grandmother said.

The old car pulled away and we were alone in what looked to me to be the middle of nowhere. I remember the tilting, gray, marker stones beneath the trees on the far side of the guardrail. My grandmother removed an ice pick and a small note pad from her purse and then steadied herself as she stepped over the metal rail. I followed. The untended graveyard was a tangle of weeds and wildflowers.

Elfleda pointed out several vines with shiny green leaves and told me they were poison ivy. She had to say no more. I knew if I didn't stay away from them it would mean a lye soap scrub-down when we returned to the house. I'd never had the scrub-down myself but had seen it done to others. With a bristle brush and a bar of her home-made soap, Fleda had been known to remove freckles, birth marks and permanent tattoos. Victims of the scrub-down were red and raw for days.

My grandmother made the soap from lye and lard. There was always a rough cut bar the color of old ivory in the laundry room. It sat on a small shelf next to the wringer and Elfleda would rub-up particularly bad spots on work clothes before putting them in the wash. It had many other uses as well.

The recipe for lye soap is a simple one – take the biggest pot you have, heat together the lard, lye and water, pour it in a pan and let it cool - but it was more an art than a science. Temperatures were critical and amounts had to be altered in accordance with the weather. The only calibration device was a small wooden paddle that hung in the laundry room and, as far as I know, was never used for anything else.

I watched her make the soap often but recall very little. Ice cubes were sometimes involved and the way the heated mixture clung to the paddle was of great importance. From time to time Elfleda would touch the tip of her tongue to the paddle. In retrospect I assume she was testing to see if the lye to lard ratio was correct. At the time it struck me as an odd thing to do because the whole operation smelled awful. I never asked for a taste. These things and the fact that there was a lion on the box the lye came in are all that I remember.

We spent the better part of the afternoon among the grave markers. My grandmother used the ice pick to dislodge lichens from the stones and wrote down names and dates in her notebook. I wandered off into the poison ivy. When she had all the information needed we returned to the guardrail to sit and wait for our ride.

Elfleda was born in 1898, the year of the Spanish American War; the year New York City annexed surrounding counties to form the five boroughs. William McKinley was president, Victoria ruled the British Empire, and Roy Bean was the law west of the Pecos. She was five when the Wright Brothers first flew at Kitty Hawk, 72 when Neil Armstrong walked on the moon and 87 when she died. It was a very long life by any standards.

My grandmother told me to listen for the cars and let her know when I heard one coming from the east. The afternoon sun pushed hard on the asphalt and satin black bubbles appeared in the cracks. I poked the bubbles with a stick and listened for cars.

In recent years the road has been straightened and the old bridge replaced but the graveyard is still there.

TEDDY BEAR'S PICNIC

I never believed in Santa Claus. There should be a time in a child's life between the dawn of awareness and the full light of logic when fantasy holds forth. It is during these years a child believes in such things as Santa, the Easter Bunny and the Tooth Fairy. It never happened for me. I did, however, fall hook, line and sinker for the Teddy Bears' Picnic.

My sister was a year older than I and in 1953, her first year at the one-room Bearsville School, I spent quite a bit of time with my maternal grandparents. The Teddy Bears' Picnic, an old British song, was popular during the Great Depression. One day my grandfather Victor remembered it and thought it would be a fun song. He sang it for me. Mary, my grandmother, who remembered the song as well, joined in.

If you go down in the woods today
You'd better not go alone.
It's lovely out in the woods today
But better you stay at home.

For every bear that ever there was
Will gather there for certain, because
Today's the day the teddy bears have their picnic

Neither Mary nor Victor was known to have a great singing voice but they made up the difference with theatrics. My grandparents danced around me like bears. They really sold the song and I bought it. There was no doubt in my mind that bears indeed held a picnic and **all** the bears would be there. What's more, they did this picnic thing on a regular basis.

Once a month my father went to Rotary meetings at Deanie's so that was pretty much my frame of reference. The bears, I reasoned, would be meeting monthly as well and seeing how this was a picnic we were talking about they would meet during the day not at night like the Rotarians. Early fall was perfect picnic weather and what better place for an all-bear picnic than Bearsville.

Teddy Bears give the impression of being warm, cuddly little creatures but the lyrics seemed to suggest otherwise. Perhaps some transformation came over them during the picnic and they turned into mean little carnivores. I later learned that a similar change occasionally overcame Rotarians at Deanie's.

As for the bears, it was my plan to heed the advice given in the song and stay out of the woods altogether whenever the bear picnic was scheduled. Toward that end I asked my grandfather, who hailed from Brooklyn, when this picnic was to be held. He didn't know and seemed to be genuinely baffled by the question. "You're not afraid of bears, are you?" he asked.

My grandmother, a product of Queens, tried to put my mind at ease. "Bears are more afraid of you than you are of them," she said. I was willing to bet the under on that one.

I asked some follow up questions but could never pin them down on just where and when this picnic was to be held. I came to the conclusion that the simple solution would have been to stay on the roads and leave the woods to woodland creatures. Simple yes, but it was not a workable solution for me. While my grandparent's house was nearly a quarter mile from my own by the road it was much less if one cut through the woods, a short par four at best. To make matters worse I was now old enough to be sent on my own from one sanctuary to the other.

My grandmother could watch me for the first third of the journey and my mother would establish visual contact upon re-entry but during the middle part of the trek I was on my own. There was a well worn dirt path to follow so getting lost was not a possibility but I would be facing fifty or sixty yards of prime bear habitat while off the grid, under the radar and out of the loop. It has been said that the Catskill Mountains have the fastest regeneration rate for foliage of any place in the country and the strip of real estate between my grandparent's house and my own was no exception.

I spent the afternoon counting the minutes like a death row prisoner and then, as I always knew it would, my departure time arrived. Grandma Mary called my mother on the phone to tell her I was coming. Next she walked me to the edge of her back lawn, yelled "Here he comes!" at the top of her voice and, without ceremony, pushed me off on my way. How could she be so cavalier with a first born grandson? If today were the day of the bear picnic I was lunch meat.

As I walked the Teddy Bear song playing over and over in my head until fear overcame me. I looked back. My grandmother was gone; orange sumac, scarlet wood vine and golden birch leaves obscured my view. In the direction of my house the forest looked like the Lions-n-Tigers-n-Bears scene from The Wizard of Oz. There was no choice but to run for it and I did so with Teddy Bears from Hell snapping at my heels.

I burst out of the forest, screaming like a banshee and wrapped my arms around my mother's legs. Regaining some composure I looked up and informed her that bears are more frightened of us than we are of them.

My mother looked down at me and smiled. "Bears must wet their pants an awful lot."

ONTEORA PART 1

My formal education began in the one-room Bearsville School. There were about 25 students in attendance but only 10 different surnames among them. The school covered K through 6. I was the K while my sister and best friend were the entire first grade.

By the early 1950's it was becoming apparent that the system of one-room school houses, so prevalent in the Catskill Mountains, was not going to hold up to the onrushing tide of baby boomers. Twenty towns, from Pine Hill to West Hurley, from Sampsonville to Woodstock, banded together to create the Onteora Central School System and build the new school in Boiceville.

I was in the first wave to hit the beach. On a warm September morning in 1954 we stepped down from the buses in front of the spanking new school smelling of petroleum products like oil paint and linoleum. In the interest of clarity I want to point out that it was the school that smelled of oil paint and linoleum. We students-to-be also smelled of petroleum products but our aromas were from hair wax and shoe polish.

At five years of age I knew nothing of fate and how quickly it could change from a doorway opening out onto endless possibilities to a sealed prison vault. If I had only know what fate had in store for me beyond that moose head portal I would have taken my Hopalong Cassidy belt and lashed myself fast to the bus seat.

My class was taught by Mrs. Vincent* who, in her exuberance, set right to work introducing us to numbers and letters and how they were used. Unfortunately, I was dyslexic, a condition virtually unheard of in 1954 or, at least, unheard of at OCS. Numbers and letters and I just did not get along very well at all. After several frustrating weeks for both Mrs. Vincent and myself, I was transferred across the hall to what was then known as the Special Class.

For me it was special indeed. We didn't have to struggle with the alphabet although Skipper Barton, one of my "special" classmates, could say it forward and backward and would, at the drop of an eraser, launch into his ABCs from either direction. Nor did we have to do battle with the base ten numerical system although Skipper could count to impossibly high numbers and would sometimes do so for hours on end. What we did was play with clay, color in coloring books, nap, wake up, put our desks in a circle and listen to stories. It was a magical time and a welcome relief from Mrs. Vincent's unintended gulag.

I got along well enough with everybody in my class but my very best friend was J.J. Jessup. We were inseparable and spent our days together making endless chains out of construction paper and edible glue or drawing with pencils as big around as bread sticks on paper so rough it had chunks of wood embedded in the fabric. We painted with tempera and rolled out clay snakes so long that their ends whipped up and down like real serpents. Life was good.

It was at the beginning of the second grade and I was starting to think that a future in academia might be just the ticket for me when I made a fatal mistake. It was a mistake from which there was no possibility of recovery.

That fall everyone in the school was given the Iowa Basic Skills test. It was like no test we had ever seen before. For starters it was not a single page but a whole booklet. And this booklet was not just filled with written questions; there were little puzzles in there as well. In many ways it was more a game than a test and the best part was it required no written answers. Responses were recorded by taking a #2 pencil and filling in small circles on a separate sheet of paper. Spelling was not an issue. Indeed, very little knowledge of the English language was required. Even the #2 pencil was supplied. I knew nothing of Iowa but it seemed to be a marvelous place.

We were told the answer sheets were to be graded by machine and, like all machines, this one had no heart. When the test results were returned and reviewed my classification was changed from "Special" to "Lazy". I was yanked from the womb of the Special class and thrust into the cold, harsh reality of the more advanced group. Life was not so good anymore.

As unpleasant as the classroom time was, the hardest part came when my class, on the way to lunch or gym, would pass the Special Class in the hall. Like Adam of Genesis looking back over the wall and into Eden, I wanted, in the worst way, to somehow find a way back into the garden. There was J.J. still sitting in that tub of butter and giving me a wry smile whenever our paths crossed.

I couldn't figure it out. J.J. had taken the same test as me, the same test we all took. I knew he was as smart as I and yet there he was still playing with clay and drawing while I was enduring mental anguish and suffering punishments for my failings. One day, as my class passed J.J.'s class in the hall, I looked beyond that smile and deep into his eyes. I had my answer. The truth struck so hard that I let out a howl of agony right there in the hallway. My old friend wasn't as smart as me, he was a whole lot smarter. J.J.

had gone in the tank on the basic skills test. That little weasel had scored low on purpose. At the tender age of seven he had figured a way to beat them at their own game. From now on his life would be all the colors that Crayola could imagine while red ink would be the only color in mine.

That next summer, J.J.'s father, who worked for IBM, was transferred. This was a common occurrence in our world. I never saw him again. Occasionally I still wonder what happened to my first school friend but I have never lost sight of the lesson he taught me. The smartest rat is not the first one through the maze; the smartest rat is the one who chooses not to run.

EPILOGUE - A few years later we all got another chance at the Iowa Basic Skills Test. I was determined it would not get the best of me again. My plan was a good one. It stood to reason that if a high score had gotten me expelled from paradise a low score could get me reinstated. I would flunk the test, like my friend J.J. had, and then just lie back and let the wings of angels transport me back to Nirvana.

It was obvious what had to be done. I would need to be seen reading the test and putting down answers and most of those answers would have to be wrong. Just randomly filling in the dots would insure me a grade in the 25% range. That should do the trick.

In order to stay above suspicion my progress would have to correspond with that of the other students. I would simply have to watch my neighbors out of the corner of my eye and turn my test pages when they turned theirs. That bit of subterfuge should keep the guards, I mean teachers, from catching on.

The test would be a long one. In addition to maintaining a believable facade I would need some sort of mental activity to maintain my sanity. To a seasoned prisoner such things came easily.

The test itself was quite extensive but the answer sheet was minimal, one page covered with rows of numbers and each number followed by four small circles. The circles were, as pointed out earlier, to be filled in with a #2 pencil in order to correspond with the correct answer or, as the case may be, incorrect answer. To minimize confusion the answer page was divided vertically by alternating columns of white and light blue.

The blue and white theme of the answer sheet reminded me of the ocean and the hundreds of little circles put me in mind of bubbles under water. I made a game of the answer sheet. An underwater scene would be drawn. The rules were few –

1) One and only one dot in every row.

2) Questions must be answered in order.

Rule #2 meant that the finished product would have to be visualized in its entirety before work began. While the bulls, I mean test monitors, were reading the direction I worked up my design. A seahorse, with its curling tail and extended spines, would reach a good many of the numbered rows. The rest could be filled in by selectively adding coral, kelp and sea shells.

It worked to perfection. I finished on time and the screws, I mean professional educators, never suspected a thing. I handed in the test and whistled on down the hall. It was just a matter of time now until my life would revert back to the joyful experience it had once been.

The test results came back showing, as you, dear reader, may well have expected, that I had over compensated. The test revealed me to have the IQ of a hay bale and nobody was prepared to believe that. My status was amended once again. I was no longer categorized as "Lazy", which I had maintained all along I was not. After all, how can anybody who was willing to routinely put out the effort I did in the interest of avoiding school work be considered lazy?

My new classification was Trouble Maker. While not flattering at least it had a ring of truth to it.

*In many cases names have been changed throughout this book to protect the innocent. In other cases they have not.

ZEN AND THE ART OF DUCK-&-COVER

It was in the second grade at Onteora Central that we met THE BOMB for the very first time. A filmstrip presentation introduced THE BOMB to our class and, although we could not have known it at the time, we would live in its shadow for most of the next decade. This filmstrip presentation seemed to be part of a government funded program designed to scare the piss out of every child in America. I'm not embarrassed to admit it scared the kidneys out of me.

In order to appeal to children the filmstrip was done partially in comic book form. Our host was Bert the Turtle. Bert, a worried and timid looking terrapin, wore a hardhat to compliment his bow-tie and shell. He went into some detail as to what we could expect if THE BOMB were to be dropped anywhere near us. First we would see a flash of light so bright that if we happened to be looking in that direction it would fry our retinas like bacon. "Don't look at the flash," was Bert's advice.

Next would come a shock wave capable of pounding the school into pieces. None of these pieces would be any bigger than a

Popsicle stick. Third in line would be a fireball burning everything in its path. Someone said the fire would be hot enough to melt the urinals. I don't remember if it was Bert or our teacher who gave us that bit of information. Lastly, like a dark curtain ending the final show, a rain of radioactive dust would fall over the scene.

We were told that one of our enemies had developed THE BOMB. There was nothing more specific than that; just that it was developed by one of our enemies. Bert's nemesis in the filmstrip was a Monkey armed with a firecracker hanging by a string from a stick. As far as I remember the monkey had no name but he didn't need one. To our young minds there was no question as to who the monkey represented and who was behind THE BOMB; the Russians were.

None of us had ever been farther east than the Duchess County Fair in Rhinebeck but we knew all about the Russians. They were evil, iron-age people with mustaches and moles. They had skipped the Enlightenment entirely and now their medieval mind-set was coupled with nuclear technology. The Russian women, who also featured mustaches and moles, looked like a cross between your great-grandmother and a Bowery Street bag lady. They wore saggy stockings, shabby sweaters and sported toothless grins. These Russians were not people to be trusted. We could expect that bomb at any time.

In an attempt to put our minds at ease, Bert went on to tell us that there were things we could do to protect ourselves in case of an attack. Children were shown on the screen ditching their bikes at the first sound of alarm and diving under bus stop benches and down cellar stairs. These children were far more clean-cut and respectable then we could ever have hoped to be. They also had nicer bikes; bikes with baskets, bells and tassels dangling from the back of the handle bar grips. I wanted one of those bikes in the worst way. My mind wandered off. I wondered what the protocol was if a person happened upon a scene where the unfortunate children had been melted along with the bathroom fixtures but the bikes were still relatively unharmed.

The filmstrip ended. At this point our teacher, who was in the first year of her profession and still relatively sane, did a very odd thing. She had us drop everything and scramble for cover under our desks. We got back in our seats and then did the same thing again. We did it several more times while she followed the second hand of her watch and counted off. This, she explained, would be our defense against THE BOMB.

Huddled beneath the desk with my knees against my chest, watching the wet spot on my pants slowly expand, I mulled the situation over. In my mind's eye were the flash, the shock wave and, most clearly of all, the melted urinals. We had been told that radioactive fallout was invisible which made it hard to visualize. Just above my head were three-quarters of an inch of Catskill Mountain maple that was meant to provide a shield against these apocalyptic horsemen. No two ways about it, if that bomb fell I was charcoal.

It was then that a strange thing happened. When I let go of all my fears and gave myself up for dead a euphoric sense of calm came over me. Seven is rather young for such an epiphany but there it was staring me in the face. It could not be ignored. I decided, if the world still existed at 3:30, to skip my homework and go out and play some baseball instead. In retrospect this new-found philosophy had a negative effect on my already anemic academic performance but it was a survival technique that had to be adopted.

Many young people in the 1950's were making much the same choice. We were given an opportunity to live our lives in anxiety and trepidation but, one by one, we were beginning to say no. The Cuban missile crisis of 1962 was the peak of nuclear terror. Defectors from the status quo went from a trickle to a deluge as millions of American teens and pre-teens, unable to take the pressure anymore, began to simply tune out. To their credit the Baby Boomers refused to become a generation of hollow-eyed insomniacs marching in response to their master's voice. By the mid 1960's that culture of atomic fear had been replaced by one of defiant joy.

BASEBALL & TV

I was about four years old when I saw my first television set. My family traveled down from the Catskills to visit some of my mother's relatives in Brooklyn, New York. They had a shingled, Georgian Revival house somewhere in the Flatbush section of the borough. There was a den down in the basement of the house. Ensconced in this room like a graven idol on a low platform was the new technological marvel. The set itself was housed in a piece of furniture only slightly smaller than a chifforobe. The screen was the size and shape of a Woolworth's goldfish bowl and ground to about the same precision.

Needless to say the picture was black and white or, more precisely, dark gray and light gray. I don't know what show was on but I remember it didn't come in very well; ghostly figures flickered across a shadowy landscape. My father held me up so I could get a better look at this milestone in the history of mankind. I was quickly bored. No kids lived in this house, just adults, and that meant no playmates and no toys. I remember the boredom of that trip more than I remember the television.

The brand of baseball played in Bearsville was every bit as primitive as that early television set. For starters we had only four players; two per side. This was fine because two players at one time were all that would fit on the small strip of abandoned buckwheat plantation we used as a field. Center field and second base were just fine. Right and left field were imaginary as was third base. Overrunning first base brought the runner in contact with a stone wall which, unfortunately, was not imaginary.

In the fall of 1956 baseball and TV met when my grandfather got his first television set. This was not the family's first set but an important milestone nonetheless because his house was far enough up the hill to receive a weak signal from the two New York City stations. This meant the World Series.

Despite the positioning of my grandfather's house, reception was still problematic. The set was to be connected by wires to an antenna on a tower that was strapped to the side of the house. The tower was nearly as tall as the white pine trees that surrounded it. With one man rotating the antenna and another adjusting the knobs on the set an image could be seen. And yet, for all the problems associated with trying to watch television in Bearsville, we knew we were far better off than the people of Phoenicia. Living down in that bowl, surrounded by mountains, they were lucky to get sunshine let alone television signals.

Weather was a major factor in television reception. Warm, humid weather was bad while crisp, winter nights were good as long as it was not cold enough to cause frost to form on the antenna. As a rule, fall was the best TV season.

Another ever-present problem was electrical interference. Thunderstorms, sun spots, the northern lights, astrological misalignment and wayward comets could mess up reception for days. A pilot talking on his plane's radio at 30,000 feet would come in loud and clear. His voice would over-ride the audio of the show you were watching. Suddenly Uncle Miltie or Ethel Mertz would start impersonating Chuck Yeager. What's more, if anybody in the western part of Ulster County so much as plugged in their vacuum cleaner the picture quality went right down the crapper.

Getting a TV was a big event in that brave new age. My grandfather's set was to be delivered on a Monday and although the age of the Monday holiday was still decades away my family planned a celebration. My mother and grandmother decided the night before what dishes they would cook for the meal and calls were made to nearby relatives. Monday was, of course, a school day and I was sorely disappointed to hear that I would be in attendance at that institution and not spending the day waiting for the new set.

To avoid a nasty hill the school bus ended its run in my grandparent's circular drive. Climbing down from the bus I was not surprised to find that my father had taken time off from work to help raise the antenna and hook up the new set. He was standing on the lawn in front of the house fine-tuning the aerial by rotating it with the aid of a length of well rope. My grandfather was in the living room. He had his head out the window but his eyes were focused back in at the set. "Better, better, good, whoa, hold it, too far, back up 3 degrees, stop, right there."

"Come on in, the game has already started," my father said.

The extended family settled in front of the Philco. "This is the Worlds Series," my grandfather explained. That bit of information was unnecessary as World Series games were just about the only ones that were televised. The game was between innings and while we waited my mother asked me who I was rooting for.

"Who's playing?" I asked.

"The Dodgers and the Yankees."

My mother was born and raised in Brooklyn and she said the word "Yankees" like she was describing an evil and a sorrow, a plague upon the earth. I chose the Dodgers. It was a good choice. The Dodgers had nicknames like "Peewee", "Duke", "Junior" and

"Sal the Barber". I knew if I was to make the major leagues, which was fully my intention, I would need a nickname as well.

It was the first baseball game I had ever actually seen being played and it was quite different from our rudimentary Bearsville brand. When the razor blade commercial ended I gave the game my full attention. This new set was a good deal smaller and the screen much larger and far more readable than its Brooklyn ancestor. I could see the field and the players if not the ball.

The score was knotted, zero to zero, and the Yankees were at the plate. One of the first few batters I watched hit a long home run to give the Bronx Bombers the lead. His name was Mickey Mantle. I had to admit that Mickey Mantle was a pretty neat name as well. The Yankees also had a guy named "Whitey, a guy named "Moose" and another named "Yogi". As far as I was concerned, nicknames just didn't get any better than "Yogi". Perhaps I was a bit hasty in choosing the Dodgers and said as much. My mother clutched at her heart.

"Don't ever quit on your team," my grandfather advised. "There are still five innings to go and this Yankee pitcher, Larson, will never last. He'll be gone before the seventh."

I stuck with the Dodgers throughout a long afternoon of fruitless prayer and bitter life's lessons learned. I would like to say that my steadfast refusal to abandon that sinking ship built my character and made me a better person but truthfully I cannot.

WINKY DINK

There was nothing on television during the day in the early 1950's. It wasn't that there was nothing worth watching, there was nothing at all unless you want to count that bull's eye, iron cross, test pattern with the Indian in full dress war bonnet. Arthur Godfry started the day with his variety show (Arthur pitched Chesterfield cigarettes until they had to cut out part of his lung). After Arthur there was nothing on the set until mid afternoon when children's programming began.

My sister was a year older than I and, by grace of birth order, the commander of the television. She would decide which shows we would watch and when. I had no problem with that. Her decisions were good ones and with only two stations available our choices were limited.

Howdy Doody was a staple. Howdy and Buffalo Bob Smith reigned over Doodyville. Howdy was a freckle-faced marionette with exactly 48 freckles, one for each state in the union. I think Howdy's freckles were the educational part of the program. Bob Keeshan played Clarabell the Clown. Clarabell never spoke but communicated by using a bicycle horn; one honk for yes, two for no. He also carried a seltzer bottle which never failed to get a laugh out of me but, then again, I've always been a pie-in-the-face kind of guy.

The show had a simple format with low production costs. With legions of baby boomers tuning in each day it turned into a gold mine. Bob Smith owned the rights to the show but Keeshan wanted a larger slice of the pie. He tried to organize the other members of the cast, J. Corny Cobb, Chief Thunderthud, Princess Summerfall Winterspring and the voice of Mr. Bluster into a union to demand a bigger piece of the action. It soon became apparent that Clarabell had overplayed his hand. He was, after all, a mute clown in full makeup and bulb nose. Keeshan was quietly replaced. We, the consumers, were clueless of this dramatic back story. Neither my sister nor I noticed the changing of Clarabell. Keeshan went on to play Captain Kangaroo but I never warmed to that character.

Beanie and Cecil were clever as was Crusader Rabbit but Funny Bunny was just about as sorry as a TV show can get. I don't want to sound unkind here but there is little else that can be said about a full grown man in a bunny suit who had to eat a carrot before he could sing. It was a little like watching a dog eating peanut butter; it may amuse you for a short while but it's a guarantee that you will tire of it long before the dog does.

Kukla, Fran and Ollie were old-world hand puppets; at least Kukla and Ollie were. Fran was a real, live woman who could have easily been another Betty Furness had she played her cards right. As time passed Fran began to age while Kukla and Ollie did not. Kukla, Fran and Ollie were forerunners of Shari Lewis, and Lamb Chop but didn't have the shelf life.

Diver Dan had severe limitations. Frank Freda, the actor who played Dan was dressed in a full deep-sea diving outfit with boots and metal helmet. The fish he encountered were marionettes and the underwater special effects were achieved by filming the action through an aquarium. Dan moved about as fast as a sea urchin and he set the pace for the show. With his face all but obscured by the faceplate of the helmet and his voice muffled Freda couldn't have been happy with the direction his career path was taking. Fortunately he learned from Clarabell's mistake and kept his mouth shut.

There was a show called Clutch Cargo. It wasn't so much an animated cartoon as it was a series of stills. I don't know how they did it but the cartoon characters had real human mouths. Swampy, Clutch's friend, was voiced by Hal Smith who would later go on to voice Owl in Winnie-the-Pooh and play Mayberry's town drunk, Otis Campbell.

Clutch and crew, with their disembodied mouths, were a bit strange but for downright freaky you couldn't beat Andy's Gang. It featured respected, gap-toothed, character actor Andy Devine in a last ditch attempt to stay in show business. The other living members of the cast were Midnight the Cat and Squeaky the Mouse. These animals seemed to be in a drugged state as they flew in tiny airplanes and played tiny violins. The two would often dance around in what I later came to know as the thorazine shuffle. The show had its moments and Andy was able to hold it together but he really needed to have a long talk with his agent.

We never missed Mickey Mouse Club. It was not a favorite of mine at first but I grew into it. At one time everything I knew about women came from the underwear section of the Sears Roebuck catalog and from Annette the Mouseketeer.

Mighty Mouse was the flip side of mild-mannered Mickey. Mighty would beat cats to the point of submission and, when they tried to flee, chase them down and beat them some more. It got to the point where I would begin to sympathize with the cats.

My sister kept the shows coming and the interest high as she explained to me just what we were watching and why. And then one morning it happened. My sister was sick, too sick to feel much like watching TV. Afternoon came and she was still not out of bed. I had to go it alone. I turned on the set and switched the dial from channel 3 to channel 8 and then back to three. Heady with power I settled on a show called Winky Dink and You, a show my sister would never have chosen.

Winky Dink was a rather simple character featuring star-shaped hair. The plots were very simplistic as well. My sister, never a minimalist, would not have tolerated the show but on this day I was driving the bus.

Every week the Dinkster would get himself into a predicament and then rely on the viewers at home to get him out. It was the first attempt at interactive television. Children were encouraged to take part by drawing with erasable "Winky Dink Magic Crayons" on the "Magic Winky Dink Screen"; a sheet of plastic held to the TV screen by static electricity. Both screens and crayons were available by sending in money to the address given at the beginning and end of the show.

A typical episode would go something like this – Winky Dink, pursued by evil in one form or another, would come upon a deep canyon or raging river. At his point he would call upon his fans at home to save his simplistic little butt by drawing a bridge. There would be a long pause while good and evil stood suspended,

41

waiting for children in living rooms everywhere to attach the screen and finish drawing the bridge.

If you didn't have the Magic Screen, which I didn't, Winky Dink would levitate across the canyon or river and the show would go on. It would go on but it just didn't make much sense. I couldn't let the Dinkman suffer such an embarrassment. I know I am not the only one who ever drew directly on the television screen with hard-core Crayolas but I was the only one my father caught.

LITTLE LEAGUE

Nothing in my life has been as real to me as Little League. I am fifty years distant from those days but there are still times when the smell of fresh cut grass can transport me back to the 1950's and back to Andy Lee Memorial Field. God was in his heaven, Ike was in the White House, smoking was good for you (9 out of 10 doctors agreed), and I was entrenched at third base. All was right with the world.

We were divided into four teams. The three New York teams were represented, Yankees, Giants and Dodgers, but the fourth team was, for some unknown reason, the Indians. What the connection was between Woodstock and Cleveland eludes me to this day. I was on the Yankees and our coach was "Hoot" Gibson.

Each team played twice a week and on game days nothing else could gain purchase in my mind. I have many memories of that time but, ironically, few of them involve the actual game itself. When the contest started everything else shut down. There was nothing in the world but the brown infield dirt, the green grass and the white ball against blue sky.

43

Once, while facing a flame-throwing twelve-year-old with an erratic fast ball and five o'clock shadow, I got a broken-bat single to right. Second base was attained by the grace of a passed ball and third via the same conveyance. I tagged up and scored on a long fly ball to shallow center but all this was meaningless. While out there on the base path my mind could focus on nothing but that broken bat. I had been the one to break it so it should, by all rights, be mine. What a trophy it would be.

Imagine my disappointment, upon returning to the dugout, to find that Jimmy John had laid claim to the bat during my unavoidable absence out on the base paths. At this point the reader might be thinking, "It's just a broken bat for, crying out loud. What's the big deal?"

I am here to tell you it was a big deal. Sporting equipment was in short supply in the Catskills in the 50's. Bats were scarce, gloves and hats sometimes had to be shared and baseball shoes were unheard of. For example, I was playing in a pair of sneakers that needed to be firmed up with cardboard and duct tape before each game. I know Jimmy John's situation was comparable. This was by no means an indictment on our folks. No parents in their right mind would buy a child a new pair of sneakers at the beginning of summer. For the most part we had to be ridden down, roped and tied for semi-formal events like Little League and we loved Little League. The rest of the time we ran wild, over the mountains and through the streams, like the aboriginals we were. Parents who bought a new pair of sneakers at the beginning of June knew full well that they would only have to turn right around and buy another pair for the start of school in September.

Bats, even broken ones, were a precious commodity in that day and age. Both of us had plans to mend the broken bat with wood screws, glue and black tape and then use it at home. We both wanted that bat.

Hoot Gibson, with the wisdom of Solomon, announced that he would flip a coin to see which one of us would get the bat. He took a silver dollar out of his pocket and waved it quickly before us. One of us made the heads-or-tails call and Hoot flipped the coin into the air. The dollar landed in the grass but neither Jimmy John nor I reacted. The coach looked at us in anticipation but we stood as statues staring down at the coin. "What's the matter," Hoot said. "Haven't you ever seen a silver dollar before?" He had struck the nail squarely on the head. Neither one of us had. We literally did not know heads from tails.

When I was eleven or twelve I hit a home run to win a game. This was a singular event for me. I was not one of the better players and it may well have been the only home run I hit during my entire career. Although unknown to me at the time it was the high point of my life. In a way it is unfortunate for one to peak so early before one is old enough to put things in perspective. A cigar and a glass of Champagne were clearly in order but that was not to be. I was taken instead to Charlie's Ice Cream Parlor and told it was my prerogative to order anything on the menu. I opted for a confection called the Pigs Delight. It was an imposing edifice; a colossus with three scoops of ice cream for a base.

I don't recall if my home run went to right or left field, what the score was or how many people were on base. None of those situational details that are of the utmost importance to the game of baseball have stuck with me over the years. Memory is an unreliable servant. I don't remember the lesser details of those by-gone days, not even who won the coin toss and that coveted broken bat. The ice cream was chocolate.

From the time the last snows of winter melted in spring and on into the early summer we used to play pick-up games in the field on the Bearsville flats across from Ernie Bark's gas station (next to where the fire house is now). It was a primitive game. We often didn't have enough players to field two entire teams and were forced to downsize, eliminating unnecessary positions like right field and catcher.

Most of the time we only had one ball and it was seldom a new one. Frequently the laces broke and the horse hide cover went flying off as the ball spun wildly across the field unraveling as it went. When this happened the game would have to stop while somebody snuck over to Ernie's garage and liberated a roll of electrical tape. It was important to get the old sort of tape that had a cloth-like surface. By comparison, the vinyl tape of today is an inferior product.

I was not a great player but a valued member of the tribe none the less. My mother was a nurse and in those days nurses didn't wear Reebok Realflex running shoes or New Balance cross trainers but sturdy leather shoes with a white finish. This meant I had access to the white shoe polish which we needed to paint the tape ball. You can see here why the old, cloth tape was preferable. The porous surface would hold the shoe polish while the newer, vinyl tape would not. A coat of the polish didn't turn the taped ball white by any means but it would bring it up to a light, smoky gray which, in turn, could extend the game an extra inning into the gathering dusk.

When Little League started up the games on the flats died down only to pick up again in the fall and go on until the weather no longer permitted such activities.

EPILOGUE - I still have Brown Beauty, the glove from my last year of Little League. It served me well throughout Babe Ruth, American Legion and then for many years of softball. It is retired now, wrapped in a plastic bag on the top shelf of my closet. The leather is cracked and worn and the webbing has been repaired many times with shoe strings and bits of wire. I get it down ever few years and rub it with neatsfoot oil. It may be the closest thing to a ritual I have in my life. While I work I can smell the leather and the oil and, if I close my eyes, I can still smell the grass.

WOODSTOCK PROPPER

Caesar said that all of Gaul is divided into three parts. Woodstock, on the other hand, has considerably more sections and sub-sections than that.

One group might be the locals or native Woodstockers. I don't know what passes for a local now-a-days but back in the era of rotary dial phones on party lines anyone whose clan had been around less than a hundred years was considered a Johnny-come-lately. The pedigree of a family with indoor plumbing was suspect. Locals were sub-divided into Dutch of Germanic origin and other Germanic peoples of Dutch origin.

Newcomers have always been an important part of the Woodstock fabric. Newcomers could, by definition, come from anywhere but for the most part they came from the New York City metropolitan area. These were often fine, upstanding folks but their families could live in Woodstock for generations and never achieve the status of local.

My father's family was a mixed bag of European extraction; English Separatists and peons of Patroons, French Huguenots, Pilgrims, Puritans and Palatines. By the beginning of the 1700's they had been run out of nearly every country in Europe. They found sanctuary in the Catskill Mountains. My mother was from Brooklyn which made me a bit of a hybrid. Most locals accepted me as one of their own but a few were reticent. After all, if your cat had kittens in the oven would you call them biscuits?

Woodstock could also be divided between people who actually lived in the village itself and those who lived in the surrounding countryside. I don't recall there being specific names for the two sub-species but for the sake of this document I will use "Townies" and "Rubes"*.

There was always considerable co-mingling of the two groups. Townies could be found hiking the Overlook or ice skating on Yankeetown Pond while Rubes frequented the movie house on Tinker Street as well as the playing fields of Rock City Road. The difference was that when Townies hung out they did it on the village green while Rubes were more likely to be found hanging out on the upper reaches of the Sawkill.

IBM employees, known as Beamers, were yet another group. Technically they were a sub-genre of Newcomers but being differentiated by the fact that they were extremely new. Nearly every Beamer categorized himself as being "Not a typical IBMer"; nearly every one of them was wrong. A wave of their children hit the Onteora Central School system in the mid-1950's. They were a good deal more sophisticated than Townies and miles ahead of Rubes. That is to say, all of them had indoor plumbing and central heat.

I hate a parade and Woodstock had one every Memorial Day. The only thing more boring than watching a parade is being in one. As a member of the town's Little League I had the honor of being in several. The parade ended at the cemetery where men in uniform would shoot guns into the air. The gunplay and the guy hiding up behind the trees and playing the bugle were the only things that made the day tolerable.

During the run-up to Christmas there was always a gathering on the village green. To me it was just like being in a very cold parade that didn't go anywhere. Things livened up when the fire truck arrived and ran the ladder up to the roof of the Dutch Reform Church. Out from behind the steeple popped Santa. He made his way along the ridge and down the ladder where he sat in the back of the fire truck dispensing stockings to all the kids. I was a bit miffed that naughty children got stockings just the same as nice ones but said nothing. Inside each stocking was a box of hard candy and an orange. The candy was worth the wait but I never could figure out what the story was behind the orange. Perhaps it was meant for the naughty kids. The Christmas gathering goes on to this day, bigger and better than ever, although the town's insurance carrier has put the kibosh on the part where Santa cat-walks across the icy roof of the church.

The high point of the year, the hub around which the social wheel turned, was the Library Fair. My grandmother always chaired one of the booths. In the weeks leading up to the fair I had to go with her to sort and price items. Every year there was always a mountain of first-line-irregular lamp shades that came from the factory up on the Bearsville flats. We sold them for pennies on the dollar. Woodstock had to be the best equipped town in America when it came to lamp shades.

On occasion my mother and one or two of her more sophisticated friends would take us to the Espresso Cafe for lunch. I always got the California burger. I don't remember just what made the California burger different from all the others but I assume it was something that spoke to the palate of that distant land. My palate was honed on frozen pot pies, fish sticks and Spaghettios and all I knew of California I got from songs by the likes of Jan and Dean. Nevertheless it was the burger I ordered.

To a Rube like myself, the town of Woodstock was an exotic place and the Cafe Espresso was the epicenter. It had a continental flair despite the California Burger on the menu. The floors were uneven and in places the finish was gone entirely from the wide wooden boards. The tablecloths were red and white. There was a long wall of windows that looked out onto the patio where tables were set up during the summer. We never sat out there; the patio was for the tourists.

The 1960's saw the rise of the poster and, as one would expect, the walls of Cafe Espresso were lined with them. Some advertised upcoming musical events but many were there to make a statement. Peace was a big topic as was Nixon. Most featured some degree of psychedelia and day-glo colors. The one that struck me the most, the one I remember to this day, said "Protest Against the Rising Tide of Conformity". This message seems so out of place in today's Woodstock, a village that is more interested in protecting property values than in registering protests, but at that time I thought it was the town's motto.

The Seahorse tavern was where the divorced women hung out. It was taboo. Married men, particularly married Rubes, were not allowed to go into the Seahorse. They went instead to the Brass Rail.

The first time I got to be downtown by myself was a rite of passage. It was an exhilarating experience. I was fortunate to have Townie friends who taught me the finer points of loitering. They showed me the best places to hide behind the News Shop when Clancy, the town's lone cop, rolled into sight. I don't recall doing anything that would put us in Clancy's cross hairs but hiding from him seemed like the thing to do so we always did it. Hiding from Clancy was a seasonal activity. He was part-time and only worked summers.

Odd characters were always in ready supply. Woodstock was heavily into the 1960's long before the decade had a chance to earn its identity. I can't say for sure that Woodstock had a village idiot. Several candidates come to mind but no one head pops above the fence line. Town drunks, on the other hand, were in such abundance that they had to take turns. They were to be avoided as well. I don't think they were particularly dangerous but they did smell bad, talk coarsely and displayed a proclivity for throwing up.

There was an older couple who drove their car down to the village green every evening after dinner. Obviously Rubes from one hollow or another where television signals did not penetrate; they always parked in the same spot, just up the street from Joe's Barber Shop. The old man rolled down the window on the driver's side and smoked. She sat in the passenger's seat and did needle point. It was their evening entertainment and they did it for years; throughout the 1950's, 1960's and beyond. They never got out of the car but were content to sit and take in the show, and what a show it was as they watched the decades pass.

* Rube Goldberg, who lived up on Cooper Lake Road in Bearsville, was not a Rube. He once bought Christmas cards from me which was particularly big of him considering the fact that he was Jewish.

ISHMAEL VERSUS THE SQUIRRELS PART 1

In junior high I read a short story called *Lenigan Versus the Ants*. I don't recall the author or much about the story other than it was about a guy named Lenigan and he did battle with an army of ants that were laying waste to the countryside in a remote part of some Latin American country. Lenigan dug ditches, flooded fields, set fires and eventually triumphed over the ants. Or maybe Lenigan lost. My memories of junior high are foggy at best.

I do, however, recall my grandfather Ishmael and his battle against gray squirrels in the summer of 1958. It was his first year of retirement and my ninth year of existence. School was out and my plans for summer were fixed. I'd found a shovel handle in the remains of the chicken house and I planned to pass my time batting rocks from the edge of the dirt road toward a line of white pines on the far side of the garden. In my own version of Home Run Derby it would be Mantle versus Aaron one day and Mays versus Killebrew the next. My plan came to an end when the phone rang just after breakfast on the first day of summer vacation. My mother answered.

"Is the boy there?" was all Ishmael said.

"I'll have him ready," my mother replied.

As the oldest male grandchild it was common for me to be pressed into service whenever my grandfather needed assistance. I knew the drill. The old man needed a second pair of hands to stack pole wood or a slender body to squeeze into the spring house and down into the icy water to free the foot valve. I usually enjoyed working with him, in no small part because he was trying to quit smoking and always had a roll of Life Savers which he readily shared, but today I did not want to be interrupted. Today the wind was blowing out at my home run derby, rock batting field. I sat despondently on the stone wall beside our driveway and waited for him to pick me up in his old station wagon.

As he cleared a place for me on the seat Ishmael explained the nature of our mission. We were to build a squirrel-proof bird feeder. Even at nine years of age I understood the squirrel-proof bird feeder was the Holy Grail of woodworking. It was a great honor to be asked to take part in the quest; batting stones could wait.

Working from a drawing he'd made on a piece of brown butcher paper we knocked out the prototype in short order. It was a conventional looking feeder made of redwood for durability with a glass-faced hopper so the seed level could be easily checked. What set this feeder apart was a row of vertical, wooden dowel rods across its face. I loved it. It made me think of one of the jailhouse windows that Poncho and the Cisco Kid were always conversing through.

My grandfather explained the principle it worked on. Small birds could poke their heads through the bars and pick up seeds while the larger squirrel heads simply did not fit. It occurred to me to ask him where he got the squirrel head needed to calibrate the bar spacing when he was making his drawing but I did not. It was probably information best kept from a nine-year-old.

Ishmael mounted the feeder on a section of well pipe driven into the ground. He chose the spot carefully; a spot where he could watch it out of the window as he drank his morning coffee. As evening fell I returned home and he retired to await first light and first squirrel.

The next morning Ishmael had a glorious time laughing at the big-headed squirrels and their frustrated attempts to filch sunflower seeds while I batted rocks till my arms ached. That night we both went to sleep proud of our accomplishments.

But in the morning our phone rang again and my mother answered. Before long Ishmael and I were back in the wood shop and back at the proverbial drawing board. It had taken the squirrels less than 24 hours to solve the puzzle. They had come in the night and eaten through the wooden dowel rods in a jail break that liberated a quart of sunflower seeds.

My grandfather was not discouraged and I was buoyed by his resolve. We set to work and soon fashioned a second feeder. This time he used steel rods in place of wooden dowel. It was back to the house and back to the well pipe. The next morning it was back to the wood shop. This time the squirrels had eaten away the wood that held the steel rods in place and once again made off with the bird seed.

At this point a lesser man would have thrown in the towel and embraced the squirrels but, as anybody who knew my grandfather would tell you, Ishmael was not a lesser man. The gloves came off and the rusty, twin barrel, twelve-gauge shotgun came out of the back of the closet.

CEMENT POND

Promethean might be a word used to describe my family. I am sure there are other words that can and have been used to describe them but for the sake of this story we will stick with Promethean.

My folks, like everybody else who ever lived, had always wanted a swimming pool. So in the early spring of 1941 they set about digging one. They had no backhoe or bulldozer but they did have picks, shovels, an old, ironed-wheeled Fordson tractor and a homemade variation of the Fresno scraper. If you are unfamiliar with the Fresno you have only to imagine an oversized wheel barrow with the long, wooden handles but without the wheel. It was pulled behind the tractor by two ropes attached to the midpoints of the two sides.

After the ground was broken up by deploying the picks and shovels, the tractor pulled the Fresno over the pile of loosened earth. Two men lifted the handles of the Fresno so the front would dig into the dirt and scoop it back into the wheel barrow shaped portion. The tractor then hauled the dirt to the dumping area with the two men trailing behind. At the dumping area the Fresno was inverted and emptied. It was then righted and the process repeated until the job was done. It needs to be pointed out that this was no small kiddie pool; it measured 20 feet in width, 60 feet in length and over 8 feet in the deep end. Digging this hole would have been considered cruel and unusual punishment or, at the very least, back-breaking work if it were not for the fact that they were doing it for fun.

When the hole was completed the sides were laid up with rocks from the quarry on the mountain behind the house and from the stream bed below the house. The dry laid stones would not hold water so the surfaces had to be covered with concrete. A ditch was dug up to a spring on the hill above the pool and a pipe installed for a water supply. It was christened with a trickle of Catskill Mountain spring water the summer before the attack on Pearl Harbor and has been, to the best of my knowledge, in constant use ever since. I came on the scene in 1948 and the pool was a part of my life from the very beginning. I cannot remember a time when I did not know how to swim.

The entire operation was primitive by today's standards. The diving board was an oak plank with a burlap bag covering the business end to prevent slipping. The floatation devises were old inner tubes; the ones from tractors were big enough to hold three or four kids. On sweltering summer nights, my parents would sometimes take us down to the pool to swim in the dark. It was magical, made better by the fact that my mother would take along a bar of soap and the late night swim would also count as our bath.

Cleaning the pool every year became the family's, Memorial Day tradition that extended out to the neighborhood. It was an unwritten law that if you were there to help clean the pool you would be able to use it all summer. There was never a shortage of labor on pool cleaning day. Nor was there a shortage of work to be done. The pool had no filter and no cover so it spent the fall collecting leaves, the winter shrouded in ice and the spring breeding frogs.

A day or two before the cleaning a brave soul would go down the embankment beyond the deep end and pull the plug from the drain pipe. Memorial Day would dawn to find the empty pool coated with a primordial soup of slimy organic matter in every form. A garden hose and stiff brooms were used to scrub down the sides and floor. Care was taken to remove amphibians in various stages of development to a more prosperous location.

When the scrubbing was complete we would all take a break to allow the sun to dry both the pool and the participants. The best part came next. Five gallon buckets of whitewash were mixed by hand and then applied with big broad brushes. Painters and pool were given a liberal coating. Older kids whitewashed the higher parts of the wall, small kids did the lower wall and then everybody did the floor. We were usually done by noon, just in time for a cook-out with hot dogs, burgers, and any number of salads none of which contained vegetables, unless you want to call macaroni or the potato a vegetable.

In May the pool's water was ice blue and ice cold but by June it had warmed both in color and temperature. By July it had changed, despite the buckets of copper sulfate that were added at regular intervals, from cerulean to sea green. After the end of July the copper sulfate did little to discourage the growth of algae but it did turn our hair an interesting tint of green. By the end of August it was pea soup and only the bravest of the lot ventured to swim in it.

By September it was all over. The pool became just another pond gathering flora and fauna throughout the long Catskill winter and waiting to be born again in the spring.

ISHMAEL VERSUS THE SQUIRRELS PART 2

In the summer of 1958, at the age of nine, I was pressed into service helping my grandfather in his quest to be the first man to build a squirrel-proof bird feeder.

My grandfather, Ishmael, was what sociologists might call a subsistence farmer. On a half dozen, steep, rocky acres in Bearsville he raised pigs and chickens and kept a milk cow. He and my grandmother, Elfleda, tended a vegetable garden on a relatively flat section of ground about half the size of a suburban lawn. My grandfather was also a housewright, a stone cutter and a blacksmith during the week. On Saturday he would cut hair on the back porch for fifteen cents a head. Today all these trades seem so outdated but back during the first half of the 20th century they were common occupations.

As far as I know Ishmael never hunted for sport but in his day a man who owned a gun and knew how to use it could augment the family food supply. Believe it or not, in the time before WWII the white tail deer was extremely rare in the Catskills but the occasional large rodent or marsupial provided a welcome change to a steady diet of chicken and pig meat.

After the squirrels foiled Ishmael's first two attempts at building a squirrel-proof bird feeder, chewing through the wooden dowels in the first one and chewing around the metal rods in the second, he rolled out the artillery in the form of an antiquated scatter gun. He was not going to have his retirement spoiled by what were little more than rats with fluffy tails.

Once again I got the call although this time it was more for moral support. The old man and old gun were not strangers but it was clear to see by the rust on the shotgun's barrels that they had not seen each other in quite some time. "If anything goes wrong you go get your grandmother," Ishmael explained. I realized then the serious nature of our mission.

My grandfather showed me how a shotgun worked and explained gun maintenance as he cleaned and oiled the 12 gauge. Next he selected two of the vintage shotgun shells by holding them up to his ear and rolling them in his fingers like they were fine cigars.

We set up our sniper post in the smoke house. He turned a chunk of maple up on end as a seat for himself. A nail keg, further back from the door, would be mine. The smokehouse hadn't been used for its intended purpose for quite some time but on a hot summer day it still smelled sweetly of wood smoke and bacon. Having never been so close to a gun that was about to be fired I waited, nervous with anticipation.

Ishmael propped the smokehouse door half open and then sat down to load the shotgun. When all was ready he removed his false teeth, wrapped them in his red and white handkerchief and placed them on a ledge. He was known to do this in times of danger. Skin and bone could heal but store-bought teeth that fit were hard to come by.

My fear and anxiety rose while the blood surged behind my eardrums. I wanted to bolt back to the safety of my home; the back of my bedroom closet to be exact. My grandfather sat between me and the door. Behind us was only the blackness of the smokehouse and a small gable vent; too small to serve as an escape route.

Ishmael was trying to quit smoking and ate Life Savers to help with the cravings. I was always happy to eat Life Savers in solidarity and at this point I needed one badly. I was just about to ask when the old man passed one back to me.

My heart rate was beginning to settle when my grandfather spoke in a harsh whisper. "There's one in the apple tree."

I leaned forward to look. Just as I did the world exploded and the smokehouse shook. Outside the door there was a spray of leaves and green apples and then I saw the squirrel, untouched, leap from the tree to the back of the redwood chaise lounge. There was another explosion and this time the thin part of the world I could see from the smokehouse door was filled with wood splinters. My grandfather kicked the smokehouse door open and cursed the squirrel as it bounded across the lawn.

When the echoes of the cursing and the gunshots subsided the world became strangely quiet, so quiet we could hear the squeak of the screen door hinges on the porch. My grandmother stepped out into the yard. Never built for speed, she walked with deliberation toward our outpost.

Elfleda stopped in front of my grandfather blocking any chance he might have of escape. She looked at the broken apple tree and then at the perforated lawn furniture and lastly down at me. When she finally did look up at Ishmael it was a look that would curdle milk.

"It's these damn bi-focus glasses," Ishmael stammered through toothless gums. "A guy never knows which section he's to look through."

Elfleda was having none of it. "You've done your last shooting," she said as she snatched the gun from his hands and turned back to the house.

At this point a prudent man would have seen the wisdom of conceding a certain portion of sunflower seed to the squirrel contingency. But, those who knew him would confirm, my grandfather could never be accused of being overly prudent.

PLANE SPOTTERS

Summertime was a glory for us. My friends and I ran over the mountains and up and down the streams with impunity. Our parents put us out after breakfast and didn't expect to see us until lunch. Sometimes, in their wisdom, they handed us a sack lunch when we left and bid us goodbye for the day. The lunch was little more than a sandwich and an apple. Streams, springs and ponds would supply our beverage. The rule of thumb for drinking water was that if frogs lived in it, it wouldn't hurt humans.

We were gone from the time school let out in June until our parole was revoked in September. Nothing could stop us with the possible exception of rain. Thunderstorms could be waited out under trees, rock ledges or bridges but a persistent rain could dampen our spirits along with every other part of our bodies.

When the skies were a universal, flatiron gray and the rain was unrelenting we were confined to the house. Usually it was my house. One day, while waiting out the tail end of a hurricane, we were driven, by the relentless force of boredom, to the bookcase.

None of us would have ventured there under any but the most dire of circumstance.

We found little relief among the tomes until one of us happened upon a small book of WWII air plane silhouettes. My father, who spent four years during the war flying C-47s in China, Burma and India, explained to us what it was. These books were used during the war to identify aircraft and separate the good from the bad. He pointed out some of the more interesting planes.

My dad went on to explain to us that during WWII there was, up in California quarry above the town of Woodstock, an observation post for spotting aircraft. Patriotic citizens would take turns manning the post and watching out for enemy planes. If any enemy craft came on the horizon they could be identified by using a book like this one we held in our very hands. The rest of the day was spent memorizing airplane silhouettes and running flash card type tests on each other.

The next morning dawned clear and bright and we were ready for action. We took our WWII surplus back pack and loaded in the plane identification book, along with ammo for our BB guns, lunches, and a pair of WWII surplus binoculars. WWII surplus canteens hung from WWII surplus web belts around our waists. As you might guess, WWII surplus items, plentiful in those days, were a big part of our lives.

All these supplies, along with our BB guns, were hauled up on the side of the mountain behind the house to set up our own observation post. My friends were convinced the Luftwaffe had our number and they concentrated on scanning the skies for silhouettes of Messerschmitts and Junkers. I wanted, more than anything, to spot a Japanese Zero. The fact that the last Japanese Zero bit the dust a decade earlier did not dampen my enthusiasm.

We had watched enough John Wayne movies to know that German and Japanese pilots could not shoot worth a fig but American pilots almost never missed their mark. Precautions would have to be taken. After all, if we shot at passing airplanes, ours or theirs, it stood to reason that they might shoot back. Bringing the combined firepower of three BB guns to bear on a wayward P38 was not a mistake we cared to make. Memorizing the silhouettes of allied airplanes seemed to be a prudent thing to do.

Having the enemy aircraft spot us first would spoil everything. To prevent such a setback several hours were spent whacking up the foliage with dull hunting knives and building a camouflaged observation post behind a stone wall. It is important to note here that this was the 1950's, before the advent of the Department of Social Services. Unescorted eight-year-olds running around the

Catskill Mountains with hunting knives and guns were a common sight. Airplanes, however, were not.

Our camouflaged position was perfect in all aspects except one. The lone window in our fortification faced a particularly dense section of woods and only a sliver of sky could be seen through the branches of a gnarly white oak. What we needed was a second observation post facing a more promising direction. More brush and low hanging branches were sacrificed for the war effort. With two active observation posts we would also need a command center to oversee operations. By this time we had denuded the immediate area and were hauling the brush that served as building materials from quite some distance. The command center did not have the elegance of the two observation posts.

With three active positions in operation communications became an issue so we connected the three posts by means of tin cans and string. This method of communication was featured on every TV science program of the day but, I am here to tell you, it is highly overrated. After talking on the tin can telephone one then had to step out of the command post and yell the message up to the intended observation post. For several hours we stuck to our positions, scanning the skies and memorizing more plane silhouettes until the lunches were just a memory and hunger drove us home.

I was recently driving down Albert Pike, not far from my home here in Hot Springs, when I saw a silhouette in the sky that looked hauntingly familiar. I followed it out to the airport and watched as an old plane landed. It was a restored B-17 stopping over on its way to an air show someplace in Texas. I was ecstatic. It had taken me over 50 years but I finally spotted one of the planes from the aircraft identification book. It was one of ours.

EPILOGUE – Not wanting to waste all the effort we put into the forts we decided, on the very next day, to use the better of them as a blind to hunt crows. Uncertain as to whether we were going to eat the crows or not, I was not entirely in favor of the plan. To me, wild game always tasted, well, rather gamey. I've eaten raccoon, porcupine, rabbit, squirrel, game birds, rattlesnake and venison cooked in a dozen ways. I'm here to tell you, none of it tastes like chicken. The fact that in the entire history of man there are no recorded incidents of crows being brought down by BB guns made it easier for me to go along with the majority.

It is a well know fact that crows hate owls. The blood feud has been going on for eons. Owls look for opportunities to punish crows after dark when the owl's superior night vision gives them the edge. Crows, on the other hand, take every chance they can get to chastise owls during the day when night vision is a curse rather than a blessing. We looked to take advantage of this long standing dispute.

My grandfather, Ishmael, had a threadbare stuffed owl that sat on a top shelf in the back of his shop. The shop was never locked and we waited for an opportunity to borrow the bird. Wednesday was double-stamp day at the Grand Union and as soon as my grandparent's car cleared the end of the lane on their way to Woodstock we had that owl.

Back up on the mountain we stowed our gear and guns in the better of the three forts and set about preparing the bait. In the middle of the small clearing in front of our fort was a sapling about 15 feet high. We bent it over like a bow and tied the owl's feet to the top with a section of our leftover phone line. When we let go of the tree, the owl sprang upright on top of the sapling in a very lifelike position.

No sooner had the owl stopped quivering when three crows came out of the trees and dive bombed the stuffed bird. In a panic we ran to the fort and spilled BBs over everything in an attempt to load the guns. By the time we were ready for any kind of action the crows were gone.

We waited and then waited some more. The crows did not return. It occurred to us that it might have been the act of the owl suddenly springing onto the scene that had drawn the crows. We pulled the sapling over, readied our guns and then let the sapling fly. No crows. With what was left of our telephone line we made a trip wire so we could release the owl while hiding in the fort. This time, as the sapling sprang back to the upright position, the head flew off the owl and landed deep in a laurel thicket.

Anybody who has spent much time in laurel thickets can tell you that they are not designed for comfort or mobility. In time we found the owl head and were able to re-attach it in a somewhat convincing manner. We made our retreat down the mountain, returned the bird to the top shelf in Ishmael's shop, powdered it liberally with sawdust and called it a day.

ISHMAEL VERSUS THE SQUIRRELS PART 3

For those new to this saga allow me to recap. In my ninth year, the summer of 1958, I was recruited by my grandfather Ishmael to join him in his war against squirrels. It was a defensive war and what we were defending was a bird feeder full of sunflower seeds.

At first we tried building a squirrel-proof feeder. Like perpetual motion and endless youth this has been a goal of mankind since the feeding of birds began. Surely, Ishmael reasoned, he could outsmart rodents. The squirrels, in short order, dispatched our every effort. Next my grandfather resorted to what could be called gunboat diplomacy except he only had an old shotgun and we fired from the smokehouse and not a boat. My grandmother, Elfleda, put an end to that tactic by confiscating the shotgun. It was a wise move on her part. Our side had sustained heavy losses in both fruit trees and lawn furniture while the squirrels remained unmarked.

Having failed at both containment and genocide Ishmael turned to deportation. What we would do, he explained to me in the coolness of the wood shop, was to build a box trap, catch the squirrels and then carry them across the valley for release. "We'll dump them over at Birg's place. There's oak trees and akerns everywhere on that ridge." My grandfather made it sound like a regular squirrel Valhalla.

We spent several blissful hours fabricating a box trap from pine board scraps, chicken wire, a sleigh bell and string. At one point Elfleda poked her head in and questioned our activities. After losing part of an apple tree and a chaise lounge to gun fire her suspicions were understandable. She left after being assured by my grandfather that we were building a wood-duck house for the pond.

When we finished he explained to me how the box trap was to work. The trap and the plan in general seemed to be infallible. I had only one question; could a determined squirrel find his way down ridge from Birg's farm, across the Sawkill and back up to our place?

Ishmael had already planned for that possibility and unveiled his squirrel identification kit. It consisted of a part can of barn red paint and an old brush. He would mark each trapped squirrel with a bit of red paint making it possible to identify returning rodents.

We baited our trap with sunflower seeds held in place by peanut butter, placed the trap under the butternut tree behind the shop and retired to the porch to wait. My grandmother pulled back the window curtains from time to time but saw only innocent checker players.

Halfway through the second game we heard the sleigh bell ring. We quickly declared a draw and adjourned to the rear of the shop. The plan was working to perfection. Through the chicken wire sides of the box we could see a furry gray squirrel, trapped yet unharmed. The beauty of the box trap was that it would also double as a carrying case.

My grandfather loaded the trap along with the paint can and brush in the back of his old station wagon, made some excuse to my grandmother and we were off for the tag and release part of the adventure.

We drove past Birg's farm and stopped on the side of the road beneath a massive oak tree. Ishmael lowered the tailgate and readied the barn paint by stirring it with the brush. Next he readied himself with one hand on the trap lid and the other on the brush handle. He lifted the brush with a dripping mass of red paint clinging to its bristles.

With a quick move Ishmael threw open the trap and lunged at the squirrel with the pain brush. The squirrel was quicker. It jumped over the brush and scurried up my grandfather's arm. Ishmael pulled back, spattering paint and turning over the bucket.

The squirrel somersaulted from my grandfather's arm and landed in the paint spill. Ishmael tried to shoo the squirrel from the car but it took off toward the front leaving barn red footprints behind. The squirrel tried the back windows and, finding them closed, clambered to the front seat. Fortunately the windows in the front were rolled down and the rodent made its escape.

The squirrel, showing no ill effects of its adventure, scurried up the oak tree. The principal casualty of this encounter had been the station wagon. Red paint was spattered throughout the back while a large puddle spread across the carpet, dripped down the crack behind the tailgate and over the bumper. Red footprints were everywhere in the back seat and oily red smears covered the windows.

Ishmael looked the situation over while he wiped the paint from his glasses and hands as best he could with his handkerchief. He cleaned a space on the tailgate and sat down. My grandfather took a new roll of Life Savers out of his pocket, opened one end and popped up the first candy ring with a thumbnail. I thought he was going to offer it to me but kept it for himself instead. He folded the foil down neatly on the rest of the Life Savers and, leaning forward, put the roll in my shirt pocket.

"Ain't no reason your grandmother has to know about any of this now is there?" he asked.

WILNA AND ROY

Woodstock was blessed with more characters per-capita than any other town I have ever known. Two of them lived just across the road from one another in Bearsville. Few people can lay claim to the title "Legend in Their Own Time" but Roy and Wilna were people who could.

Roy Oakley had a small, one-pump gas station and garage on Route 212 above the Bearsville store. It stood roughly where the town garage is today. Despite the difference in their ages (Roy was a good deal older) he and my father were friends. We always bought our gas there and I loved it. The garage was a small wooden structure with one service bay and office attached. Roy lived in a few small rooms off the back.

The building, and indeed the property around the building, was a cacophony of gathered and scattered objects. Car parts from every era dating back to the dawn of motor vehicle travel covered the landscape. Some parts went back even further to the days of horse and buggy. Sheds, lean-tos and outbuildings were everywhere; all were overgrown and sagged beneath the weight of time. All, at least to my young eyes, held treasures. Paths wound among the piles of fortune, through the undergrowth and down toward the creek. The whole place had the ambiance of a sunken pirate ship or a Mayan tomb waiting to be discovered. I wanted to live in a place like Roy's.

In his own special way Roy catered to the tourist trade. This was a source of amusement to people who knew him because they also knew that he disliked tourists intensely. He sold antiques, collectables, bluestone pavers, pumpkins, and potted plants; whatever came his way. His one pump was a thing of beauty in its own right. It had a dial for a face and was topped with a glass globe sporting the brand name ESSO. It would be worth thousands of dollars in today's collectables market. As cars came equipped with bigger, more powerful engines the need for high octane gas grew. Roy only carried regular and his friends urged him to put in a second pump.

"Why on earth would I want to do that?" Roy asked.

"So people can have a choice."

"They have a choice now," Roy explained. "They can buy my gas or they can go someplace else."

Roy was said to have been an excellent mechanic but when I first came to know him he had given up the trade. No one knew for sure why Roy quit working on cars. One day he just said that he had had enough. Legend has it that he carried his mechanic tools up onto the bridge over the Sawkill and threw them in. I do not know if that is a true story or not but I have a story of my own that might speak to the matter.

One day I was riding with my father up the Bearsville flats when we passed a pre-war sedan parked by the side of the road. "That's Roy's car," my father said. In a short while we came upon a solitary figure walking. "And there's Roy."

We picked Roy up and my father inquired as to the condition of his car. "Distributor vibrated loose and threw the timing way off," Roy said.

"I have a screwdriver in the glove compartment. We can go back and fix it," my father offered.

"You can do what you like but I don't work on cars anymore," Roy said.

I first became aware of Wilna Hervey in the 1950s. She was hard to miss, being close to six feet six inches tall and just about the biggest person I had ever seen, man or woman. Wilna and my grandfather Ishmael were good friends and she, along with her companion Nan Mason, would often come to sit in chairs out on the front lawn and visit. The women were successful artists at that time but had weathered the great depression as house painters. Ishmael had sometimes found them jobs. I tried to picture these two climbing ladders with buckets of paint but couldn't.

My grandmother, Elfleda, always did her sewing on a treadle machine. She had plenty of opportunity to modernize but never cared to. At one point repair parts for her old Singer became almost impossible to find or fabricate. Wilna heard of Fleda's predicament and offered a machine she had in storage. My grandmother was delighted. Wilna's machine was a Singer 201-K. The 201-K was introduced in 1936 which meant that Fleada had been wanting one for over 30 years. It was a win/win situation. My grandmothers machine was much older and esthetically more valuable as an antique, which was how Wilna and Nan viewed it.

I loaded my grandmother and the old machine into my van and drove down to where Wilna and Nan lived among the hemlocks under the hill. It was not to be an easy swap. The machine we were after was in storage above the garage. I unloaded Fleada'a machine and muscled it up the steep, narrow, wooden stairs. I worked alone as my grandmother and Nan were a bit too old to be doing stairs unless absolutely necessary, and Wilna, although a very strong woman at one time, was reduced to walking on two canes.

There was quite a bit of room in the loft above the garage and it was packed with the most marvelous things. I felt like Howard Carter looking into Tut's tomb. Along with the usual objects collected by older women, were props and posters from the early days of silent movies. There were bowler hats, top hats and one hat that sported an artificial sunflower the size of a dinner plate. Everything was over-size from umbrellas to handbags and suitcases. The movie posters featured Wilna as a much younger woman. She was one of the stars of a series called the "Toonerville Trolley" and was featured lifting things like safes, telephone poles and the trolley itself.

I brought the replacement sewing machine down and loaded it in the van. The three old women stood by the door to the garret. They made no attempt to break up the clutch. "Could you do something for us?" Wilna asked. "We were wondering if you could bring a few things down for us to look at," Nan added. It was obvious that neither of them would ever make it up the attic stairs ever again. There was no way I could refuse. I spent the next hour going up and down the stairs bringing down one item of movie history for their inspection and then returning it back up only to retrieve another. They told me stories of the objects and how each related to the days of silent movies. Sadly, I remember none of those stories.

FIREWOOD

We heated our house with wood; almost everybody we knew did the same. The house was a small one, less than 1,000 square feet, with a wood furnace in the cellar. There was no duct-work to move the hot air from the furnace to the various rooms. A single two-foot-square iron grate in the hallway in the middle of the house provided the sole source of heat. On cold winter nights my father would stack as much wood as he could into the fire box and damp down the air intake as much as possible. Despite his efforts the wood was exhausted and the fire always went out before morning. The house was cold.

I awoke on such mornings, curled in a ball with my head under the covers, and listened for the sounds of my father in the cellar starting the fire for the day. Next to my bed was a small wooden chair where my mother would lay out my clothes for school. When I was sure the fire had taken I would leap from my bed, grab the chair and clothes and then dash into the hall. There, ensconced over the heating grate like a skid row wino, I dressed for the day. I would have taken my meals there as well but my father, returning from the basement, would propel me toward the kitchen and then fuss while he worked to free the legs of the small chair from the grating. It was our customary morning ritual from the end of October until the middle of April.

A few people had central heat but, for the most part, my family's morning routine was repeated in houses from Bearsville to Big Indian. We would get on the school bus every winter's morning with the sweet smell of wood smoke clinging to our hair and clothing.

Cutting, hauling, stacking, burning and cleaning up after firewood was a year-round job but it was at its peak in the fall. Making wood was an extended family affair with both my two uncles and every cousin big enough to tote a chunk of wood involved. We cut for the three households as well as my grandmother and our wood shop. For a Catskill mountain winter that represented a lot of BTUs.

A 20 acre plot of land on the mountain behind the house provided a steady supply of hardwood for our fires. We cut on that steep hillside for generations but never seemed to make any headway. The last time I saw the wood lot it was as verdant as any other part of the Catskills.

We literally cut thousands of trees over the years and almost all of them fell without incident; almost all but not all. Occasionally a tree would do something surprising and those are the ones we tend to remember. In fact, when the members of my family gather and the talk leads around to firewood, which it inevitably does, it is those few rogue trees that get recalled.

Sometimes a tree would fall only a short distance and then hang up in the branches of another tree. When this happened the lumberjack aspirant had to cut the second tree as well. This cutting could only be done by squatting in the very place the first tree was going to fall when the cut was completed. Timing, good footing and a clear path of retreat were essential. There were times when the second tree, as it fell, would hang up in a third and the trees would form a chain like elephants in a circus. When such was the case it was prudent to retreat and hope that a strong wind would come up in the night and rectify the situation.

Occasionally, but rarely, a tree will do what we called "jumping the stump". This is when a tree is cut free but instead of falling it hops off the stump hitting the ground in an upright position. A tree is normally notched and then angle-cut to ensure it will fall in the desired direction but when one jumps the stump all bets are off. Such a tree can turn around and fall just as pretty as can be right in the intended spot or it can turn on its axis and chase a man down the mountainside. We never lost any personnel in this manner but did lose a chainsaw and part of a jeep.

One tree we were trying to fall into the parking area behind our shop tangled in unseen grape vines. If the tree had been bigger or the vines smaller the story would not be worth relating but as fate would have it the vines and tree worked together with precision. The tree dropped to a 45 degree angle and then bounced once or twice as the vines pulled it up short of its intended target. Everything froze for a second and then the tree began to swing around like the boom on a ship. It moved slowly at first but quickly began to pick up speed. We scattered like cockroaches in the blinding glare of the kitchen light. The tree swept around and peeled 6 feet of fascia board and two rows of shingles from the shop's overhang, took out a window and crushed a 55 gallon barrel of kerosene.

As the 1950's gave way to the 1960's the wood furnaces began, in turn, to give way to oil burners. The Rose clan made the conversion during that period. My father cut holes for heat registers in every room and patched in the hole where the central grate had been. The house stayed warm all night and getting out of bed was not such a challenge. And yet, the smell of oil heat cannot invoke memories like the smell of wood smoke does.

EPILOGUE - I have two fireplaces in my house here in Arkansas. From time to time, during our comparatively short winters, I will give in to my wife's requests and build a fire. I will never be seen handling firewood of my own free will. The exercise has long ago lost its charm.

ONTEORA PART 2

I spent my grade school years being promoted, in large part, because the Onteora brain trust could think of nothing else to do with me. When it comes right down to it school is about sorting out the horses, mules and oxen and fitting each to the proper plow. When given a particularly fast horse, smart mule or strong ox the system knows how to respond but throw an okapi into the mix and the system falters. Having been promoted from first to second grade and then on to third I had built up a certain momentum that carried me on like a bit of flotsam on a wave.

This more-or-less free ride I was getting came to an end in the sixth grade when my teacher, Miss Olin, took an entirely different view of the matter. Miss Olin was born about the same time that Van Gogh stumbled into the corn field, pistol in hand, intent on taking his own life. I am not suggesting that Vincent's despair was, in any way, connected to the birth of Miss Olin, I just intend to illustrate that there was nothing "new school" about that old masterpiece of a school teacher. Each day she brought with her two quart-sized mason jars filled with a clear brown liquid from which she shipped at regular intervals. We all assumed it was tea but, in retrospect, it might have been bourbon.

It was always my plan to use the summer to try and forget all the things I had learned in school the previous year. My reasoning being that the new teacher would appreciate the tabula rasa she was presented with in September. Miss Olin did not. It was to be her last year but, as she explained to me, she had taught my father and was looking forward to breaking one last bronco, or okapi as the case may be, before heading for pasture herself. Miss Olin was a pioneering proponent of "tough love" although the love portion of the equation was not evident to me at the time.

Her plan was a simple one, she would use peer pressure to enhance my performance. Once a day the old dear would call me to the blackboard to grapple with a bit of sentence structure or wrestle a math problem. She would then invite the class to join her in the ridicule that followed my inevitable blunders. The theory being that I would learn to perform rather than face embarrassment in front of my classmates. Like many good theories this one proved to have no practical application.

It was tough going at first but I hung in there. By Halloween my endurance was beginning to pay off and by Thanksgiving she was only bringing me to the board once or twice a week. It was becoming clear that Miss Olin's heart was no longer in it. When I returned, unreformed, from Christmas vacation the old lady threw in the towel. She banished me and my desk to the back of the room and proceeded with the remainder of the school year as if I didn't exist. There was no blame to be had here. On any given day Miss Olin had 35 or 40 other children in the classroom and they were, to varying degrees, eager for her teachings. The beginning weeks in exile were difficult ones but, like any prisoner in solitary, I learned to survive.

Classrooms in those days were fairly austere. There was a blackboard in the front of the room which sometimes had chalk and sometimes not. Above the board were portraits of George Washington on one side, Eisenhower on the other and a small American flag in the middle. The pictures of Eisenhower stayed up throughout the administrations of John Kennedy and Lyndon Johnson and, for all I know, may very well be there yet. In the back of the room, sharing my own personal Elba, was a shelf holding a set of encyclopedias with only a few volumes missing. These were beautiful old books with embossed art deco covers. You couldn't say they were current - they left World War One as a toss-up - but they were filled with finely drawn illustrations.

I got hold of a good #2 pencil and pinched several sheets of unlined paper from the school mimeograph room. I would wait until Miss Olin turned to write on the blackboard and then, taking one of the encyclopedia's volumes from the shelf, slip it into my desk. The rest of that day, and almost every day for the remainder of the school year, were spent looking through the encyclopedia reading the occasional entry and copying the illustrations.

I even got so bold as to stop in other classrooms before the first bell in the morning and, using Miss Olin's name, borrow the volumes missing from my set. Crayons, colored pencils and gum erasers were liberated from the art cart if it were parked unattended in the hallway. When the encyclopedias grew tiresome I would bring in objects from the playground and set up a small still life in my desk to work from.

Every few weeks Miss Olin would lumber to the back of the classroom with the wastebasket in hand and make me throw my art work and supplies in the trash. It was disappointing when this happened but, like any respectable, street corner drug dealer, I was soon back in business.

These were tough lessons to learn but necessary ones. Not only did I become a font of useless information and develop my drawing skills but other, more valuable, lessons were learned as well. Art is a solitary pursuit and anybody who can't handle the solitude should find another profession. An artist also needs a thick skin. If you have trouble dealing with criticism, ridicule, and verbal abuse you should consider another line of work. By the end of the sixth grade I had a hide like a rhinoceros and could easily work five or six hours a day on solo projects.

An artist should never fall in love with his or her work, it stifles creativity and growth. I never read Pygmalion but Miss Olin, through the use of frequent purges of my desk, found a way to teach me that lesson as well.

By the time the year ended I had a sound foundation on which to build a career in art. All this came to me courtesy of Miss Olin and I truly regret not having the presence of mind to thank the old sweetheart while the opportunity was there.

BEAR HUNTING WITH A SWITCH

My father Malcolm may well have been the bravest man I've ever known. He weathered the great depression, fought in World War II and faced down the Russians in the Cold War. However, these early acts of courage paled in comparison to what he did in 1963. In the summer of that year he loaded his family into a secondhand Studebaker station wagon and started out on a summer-long road trip that would take us from the Catskill Mountains to California, up the coast to Oregon and back, once again, to our home.

In the 1950's Americans owned three out of every four cars in the world and they were the biggest, most powerful cars ever built. People had jobs with good pay and vacation time. Highways and super highways were being built everywhere. The family road trip was a natural result of all these factors coming together and it became almost a birthright of the Baby Boomers.

My father bought a small, two wheeled, box trailer about five or six feet square. He built an aerodynamic top for it to keep our gear dry. It had little doors on the sides. Behind one of the doors was the bulky metal ice chest. From the drain on the bottom of the ice chest a two foot section garden hose carried the water from the melted ice out and beyond the edge of the trailer. I describe his drainage system in detail because it is, as you shall see, an important element in this story.

We began our journey on the Pennsylvania Turnpike and ended up on the New York State Thruway but in those days four-lane, limited access highways were the exception rather than the rule. For the most part we drove on two-lane roads and filled up at service stations that pumped gas and fixed cars rather than selling Lotto tickets and junk food. We ate at dairy bars with 12 foot high ice cream cones on the roof and, when we weren't camping, spent the night in motels that sported all manner of blinking neon signs. My favorite stops were at those roadside attractions my parents disdainfully called "tourist traps". My sister, brother and I were each allotted so much "rubber tomahawk" money weekly. Mine was always gone by Monday or Tuesday at the latest.

Every campground, motel pool and roadside attraction was swarming with children and they were all on the road just the same as us. It was a moveable feast. It was possible to make a new friend at the campground in the Sand Hills of Nebraska and see them again, days later, at a hamburger stand in New Mexico or weeks later in a line at Disneyland. In the Bad Lands of Dakota you might meet a friend you hadn't seen since Dinosaur National Monument in Utah and trade a giant pine cone you picked up along the road to Yosemite for a lava rock from Crater Lake in Oregon.

In about the fifth or sixth week of our travels we set up camp in Yellowstone. At that time the bears and tourists mixed freely and in short order a good-sized black bear sauntered into our campsite with mischief in her heart. With the exception of my father our family took refuge in the car. Malcolm, determined to defend his turf, picked up the two foot length of garden hose we used to drain the cooler and smacked it loudly against the fender of the trailer. "Go on, git," he shouted.

The bear rose up on its hind legs. This wasn't her first rodeo, she had been dealing with tourists since she was a cub. Hit them early was the best plan, before they learned the ground rules and how best to secure the coolers and other food stuffs. Come in big, get your bluff in and waltz off with the hot dogs or baloney.

"Git, I said," my father repeated in a tone that suggested that this would be the bear's last warning. The bear looked into Malcolm's eyes, the eyes of a man who had spent endless weeks confined in a compact car with his family. Here was a man who no longer knew fear. Such a man might even welcome death. The bear backed down. I had heard that tone in my father's voice before and, I must say, the bear made a wise decision.

Every day we saw hitchhikers. Some were young college students while others were grizzled old hobos. I was not enthralled by Kerouac wannabees but, for some reason, the hobos fascinated me. I wanted my father to stop and pick them up. He declined saying that with five of us already in the car there just wasn't room. He was right about our lack of room and he was also right, although I did not realize it at the time, about not picking up the hobos.

One hitchhiker haunts the corners of my mind to this day. We first passed him in Ohio on our second day of travel. He was dressed in a brown, double breasted suit, the kind that was always featured in film noir movies of the 30's and 40's. He even had the hat and shoes to go with it and looked a little like Humphrey Bogart on a bad day. He sat on his worn, leather suitcase by the edge of the road with a trench coat slung over his shoulder.

His hitching style was understated. He was rolling a cigarette as we approached and glanced up from his work as if annoyed by the interruption. His only concession was to raise one thumb as he held the cigarette to his mouth to lick the seam. He was in need of a shave and his eyes, dark beneath the brim of the hat, seemed to

·

focus on me. I was transported, if only for a moment, into the Twilight Zone. It was almost as if I knew him and he knew me.

That night we stopped somewhere in Iowa and my father, sister and I set up the tents for the night while my mother started dinner on our Coleman stove. In the morning we broke camp while my mother made breakfast.

It was just past noon and somewhere in the middle of Nebraska that we passed the man with the suitcase again. He looked up from his seat on the old brown satchel but never favored us with as much as a nod. He seemed to know his destiny and that it wasn't with us. Again I looked into his eyes. He seemed to know my destiny as well.

We spent two day in the Rocky Mountains and then came down into Utah and the great basin. The wind was blowing and a warm drizzle fell on the windshield. The town of Salina was little more than a glorified crossroads. The man with the brown suitcase stood on the corner where Highway 50 turns to the west. He was wearing his trench coat with the collar turned up against the weather. He was going west while we were heading south into canyon country. I waved to him as we passed and he gave me the thumbs up sign.

I have spent my life making art and traveling the back roads looking for subject matter. I have also spent my life at, or below, the poverty line. There were times when everything of value that I owned could be put into one suitcase and yet I never gave myself over entirely to the road. Today my house is full of furniture and my driveway full of cars. Inside the house, in the back of a closet, sits an old, brown leather suitcase.

BASKETBALL JONES

Those aging baby boomers who remember the golden age of Woodstock basketball may remember me as well. My star wasn't one of the brightest in the pantheon but I took to the court and sounded my barbaric YAWP along with the best and the rest.

One bright afternoon, near the end of my thirty year round-ball career, I was sitting in the portable bleachers preparing to enter the mix. I laced up the supports that added a measure of stability to my ankles. Next in line came the brace that eased the pain from the torn meniscus in my knee. As I adjusted the neoprene sleeve on my arthritic elbow I noticed a teenage girl watching me.

"Why do you play if it hurts so badly?" she asked.

It was a question that needed to be answered for her sake as well as mine. "Do not go gently into that good night. Rage, rage against the dying of the light." I quoted.

"What's up with that?" she asked.

"It's part of a poem by Dylan Thomas," I explained.

"Who's he?"

"A Welsh poet noted for drinking himself to death in Greenwich Village back in the 1950's," I said in an attempt to impress this ingenue. "It is said that poems by Thomas inspired the young Robert Zimmerman to change his name."

"What did he change it to?" she asked.

"Why, Bob Dylan, of course."

"Who's he?" she said trumping all my aces.

"Sharks gotta swim or they die," I said as I hobbled out onto the court.

My long basketball odyssey started innocently enough in early November of 1963. Rumor had spread that there was to be a seventh grade basketball team and that team was going to play games against other schools.

I did not own a basketball, I'm not sure if I had ever even held one, but to pass up an opportunity to travel to such exotic lands as New Paltz, Marlboro and Roundout Valley was unthinkable. Many others felt the same.

For lack of a better venue those wishing to be a part of this endeavor assembled in the gym of the brand new Bennett school. It was a dreary Monday afternoon but our spirits were high as we stood against the wall inhaling fumes of newness.

Whispers spread up and down the line that the school only had twelve uniforms. I leaned out and counted the hopefuls. There were twenty-five.

In short order the coach arrived with a basketball under his arm and a whistle around his neck. He lined us up for calisthenics. After half an hour of sit-ups, squat-thrusts and jumping jacks we were set to running around the perimeter of the small gym like so many hamsters in a cage. Half an hour of this and it was off to the showers. The coach retired to his office, the ball unbounced, the whistle unblown.

While waiting for the late bus I saw the coach on the way to his car. "There sure are a lot of guys wanting to play basketball," I said.

"That's good," he said.

"You're going to have to cut some people aren't you?"

The coach stopped and looked down at me. "I don't think so."

The next afternoon there were only about twenty wannabees present in the gym and we went through much the same routine; floor exercises, running and then showers. This pattern continued throughout the week and by Friday the numbers had shrunk to twelve. The coach blew his whistle for the first time and the basketballs were rolled out onto the floor.

I don't remember being much of a contributor that first season, more a warm body to fill a slot while one of the better players rested. But, in our first game I found myself alone under the basket and in possession of the ball. I threw it up toward the basket and in it went. I was hooked. I had a Basketball Jones that would ride my back for the next three decades.

For those of you not familiar with the term Basketball Jones allow me to give an example – Less than a week after the occasion of my first field goal an announcement came over the school's speaker system. Although it was still early in the afternoon we were all to return to Home Room immediately. Our home-room teacher informed us that John Kennedy, the president of the United States, had been assassinated. The buses were being sent for and we were all going home early to be with our families.

A hush fell over the room and the teacher asked if there were any questions. One student wondered if we were going to get a new president. The teacher explained the line of succession. A tearful girl wanted to know what would happen to Caroline and little John John. The teacher said we would all pray for them as such things were allowed in schools in those days.

After a long reflective silence I raised my hand. The teacher nodded in my direction. "Does this mean that basketball practice is canceled?" I asked.

WHITE PINE

Not every tree we cut was for firewood. Sometimes we had to take down one of the white pines which favored the rocky, well-drained soils of the Catskills. If given their head they would soon have taken over every field and valley. Most of the trees we cut for wood were oak, hickory or maple. They were seldom more than 18" in diameter and no more than 30 or 40 feet high. The Eastern white pine (Pinus Strobus), tallest tree this side of the Rocky Mountains, was a different matter entirely.

It has been said that Asian bamboo can grow two feet in a twenty-four hour period while trapping sleeping birds in a living cage. Once, while checking out in the supermarket, I read that Mississippi kudzu can increase its length by the rate of a foot an hour, strangling piglets and threatening the newborn. I don't know if any of this is true but a white pine can easily grow a foot a year and keep up that pace for 100 years. And what's more, this foot per year is not hollow fishing rod or flimsy vine but solid wood, bark, and pitch with heavy branches weighted down by thousands of needles.

The white pine figured heavily in the history of the Hudson Valley. In the 1600's England needed tar and pitch to service the ships in its ever growing navy and merchant fleets. Provisions from continental Europe were unreliable due to wars but the forests of the New World seemed to offer an endless supply. To meet British needs, thousands of Palatines were gathered up in Holland, shipped from England and settled in the Hudson Valley to gather pine pitch. The white pine proved to be a poor supplier of high quality pitch. The enterprise never flourished but towns like West Camp and Germantown remain from that era. The descendants of those people, my relatives included, remain as well. This love-hate relationship between the people and the white pine has been going on for centuries.

A prime example of Pinus Strobus stood on the edge of the field below my father Malcolm's house. White pine makes poor firewood. It burns too fast, too hot and leaves deposits of pitch in the chimney flu. Mostly they were cut for lumber but sometimes a tree had to be removed because it cast shade on the garden, kept the ice from melting off the driveway in the spring or threatened the well-being of the community. This tree below my father's house did all three.

The pine in question had needed to come down for quite some time but we had been putting it off. The tree had taken advantage of our procrastination and was now almost four feet in diameter and topping out at 80 feet or more. It was not going to be an easy job. To ensure success we would need all hands on deck, my father, brother and me, as well as our old Oliver tractor.

About 15 feet from the ground the tree forked. The two prongs, each as big as the lesser trees that surrounded it, ran on up for another seventy feet. The tree looked fairly straight but with the two heavy sections above the fork it was impossible to say for sure which way it wanted to fall. If it came down in the field it would be a walk in the park. We would fall on it with axes and chainsaws like the crew of the Pequod on the corpse of a whale. But if it went any other way, toward the road, spring house or the power lines for example, trouble was waiting.

A large tree made of soft wood like white pine presented certain problems that a hardwood did not. With a tree, forked like this one was, the problems could be great. The cut at the bottom, intended to fell the tree, could cause the trunk to "shaft", split vertically up the trunk, separating at the fork. The two sections could then go in unpredictable directions. We ringed the tree about 5 feet from the ground with a section of heavy chain and tightened it with a binder. This would keep the tree from shafting.

Although we never talked of it we all knew this to be dangerous work. Chainsaws were sharpened and filled carefully with gas and bar oil. I overfilled the oil reservoir on one of the saws and ran oil out and over my boot. The tractor and rope would be used to pull the tree in the direction we wanted it to go. Just about anybody in the family could drive the tractor but my brother enjoyed it the most so we let him handle the task. Malcolm would never let anybody else run the chainsaw while he was around so that left the job of chain monkey to me.

The chain monkey is the one who gets to climb up into the tree and tie the pull rope. I coiled about 20 feet of stout rope around my shoulder and started up onto the first limb. Progress was slow and painful made even more so by the spilled bar oil on my boot. Most people consider career changes from time to time and I am no exception but chain monkey would never make my short list.

I made it above the fork and worked the rope around the two sections. This would keep the pressure from the tractor from splitting the tree. For good measure I pulled up more rope and worked it around again. There was about 10 feet left so I tied a series or creative knots. When I got back down my brother had the other end of the rope hooked to the tow bar of the tractor. My father stood at the base of the tree revving his chainsaw.

"Are you sure this rope is long enough?" my brother asked as he looked the situation over.

"Plenty of line" my father said. "That was a hundred-foot coil and this tree can't be much over seventy feet high.

There were some things that just didn't sit right about that statement; "It was a hundred-foot coil"' and the tree "can't be much over seventy-five feet," for example. I kept my mouth shut not wanting to ask the kind of questions that might show lack of confidence in the outcome.

Malcolm started the chainsaw and began to cut the notch on the side of the tree toward the field. When he finished the second cut of the notch I took the back of the ax and knocked the wedge free. My father went around back of the tree, the side away from the tractor, and started cutting down on an angle that would eventually meet the notch. Between the notch, the rope and the tractor the tree should drop right on the mark.

My brother worked the old tractor into gear, let out the clutch and eased it down the field. The slack came out of the rope and small branches snapped as the noose tightened around the twin trunks up in the tree.

The rope was straining and the top of the tree shook as my father backed away from his cut. "You all set?" he shouted.

"I still don't think this is long enough," my brother shouted in reply and pointed toward the rope with his thumb.

Deafened by the noise of the saw and tractor, Malcolm returned the thumbs up sign with a smile and bent once again to his cut. I backed away to give the drama plenty of room to play itself out.

My brother set the throttle on full open, let the clutch out and, leaning back, looked over his shoulder at our father. There was a snapping of limbs, a quiver and then a sound like the earth splitting open as the massive pine started down toward the tractor.

My father stepped back and looked from the tree to the tractor. Even at a distance I could see his eyes widen and his mouth go slack. It was obvious now that the rope was somewhat shorter than the tree was tall.

My brother put one hand on top of the steering wheel and the other on the rear fender and swung himself out of the seat and free of the tractor. His feet hit the ground in a staggering run which lasted for two or three steps before turning into a drop and roll that put me in mind of the trained Russian bears from the Ed Sullivan show.

The giant pine came down and splintered around the old tractor completely covering it. The earth beneath me shook and the air that blew past my face was filled with dust, dried leaves and pine needles.

The old Oliver was not fazed. It chugged its way out of the canopy of pine boughs and, lacking a pilot, defined a short arc across the field and into a brush heap where it stalled out.

Malcolm walked up, laughing so hard there were tears in his eyes. My brother dusted himself off, inspected an abrasion on his elbow, and gave my father a dark look.

We all went over to the tractor. The right fender, the one my brother had used for a pommel, was hanging by a single bolt. The steering wheel was badly bent. "Now that you mention it," my father said. "I guess maybe I did take a few feet off that rope last summer for something. I can't, for the life of me, recall what for."

I thought it best to bid my farewells while they were still debating cause and effect. Surely it would be prudent for me to be gone before they got in amongst the branches and found my generous looping and knots.

UNCLE CHUCK & THEM

I was very fortunate to have worked with my family who were all fine craftsmen and teachers as well. I learned not only carpentry but many other things in the bargain. In the spring the talk was always about the much anticipated vegetable gardens. Garden folklore was always my favorite part of these conversations. Corn was to be planted when the leaves on the white oak tree were the size of a squirrel's ear. It should be knee high by the Fourth of July. Above ground vegetables were to be planted during the phase of the full moon while tubers were to be planted in the dark of the moon. Potatoes were to be planted on Good Friday and cucumbers on the second day of June before breakfast and before talking to anybody.

These were the days before cable TV and the Weather Chanel. We worked outdoors most of the time so predicting weather by reading signs was important. Mares tails - high, wispy clouds that turn up on the end - were a sign of rain as was a wind that exposed the bottom side of the leaves on a maple tree. Rain with the sun out, fog going up the mountain or bubbles on the puddles meant rain again tomorrow. Woolly bear caterpillars were a predictor of winters length and severity as was the thickness of a squirrel's fur. A sundog - formed by high altitude ice crystals - meant snow within 24 hours. A red sundog meant a lot of snow. A snow storm with big flakes was not one that would last long.

A lot of the signs were indicators of precipitation in one form or another but there were also indicators of fair weather. Crows cawing in winter was a harbinger of a thaw. A clear, blue sky meant no rain for three days. When the crescent moon was tipped over on its back, like a bowl, it would not rain until the moon came back up and spilled out the water. All signs were said to fail in a drought.

On most days I worked with Donald and Durand, my twin uncles. They had served in the 82nd airborne during WWII, fighting their way from Belgium to Berlin. In the process they had opportunity to dig foxholes across half the continent. Whenever we dug a footing some place in town they compared and contrasted the dirt of that particular locale to some part of Europe. While in the 82nd their lives often depended on identifying an approaching aircraft quickly. It was a hard habit to break and even in the 1960's the two would stop whatever they were doing and watch when a plane went over. "Relax," I finally told them. "They're all ours."

Uncle Chuck was one of the most interesting characters I have ever met. Just to set the record straight, Uncle Chuck was not my uncle and his name wasn't Chuck. His name was Walter Shultis and he was my grandmother's cousin. He was not only a talented carpenter but a first-rate stone mason as well. He had worked stone for so many years that his long, powerful fingers were without prints. Walt could have robbed a bank without gloves.

In the early 1960's he retired from the family construction business but still worked for a few months each summer. This was just about the time I was old enough to get working papers and I was also on the job during the summer. Walt and I would often spend the day together. Walt supplied the knowledge and craftsmanship while I went along for muscle.

We would ride to the job site together in his old sedan. My first task would be to carry Walt's hand-made, wooden tool box from the trunk of his car. There was no tape measure but a brass jointed measuring stick that folded out like a Chinese screen. There was also a hammer, two hand saws, one for ripping and one crosscut, a brace and bits, plumb bob and several other tools of the sort one might see in a modern Smithsonian display. There was not a power tool in the lot but the hand tools he had were of the finest quality and razor sharp. He would hone a chisel until he could run it along his thumb nail and curl up a shaving.

While Walt was a talented craftsman he was a gifted musician. There is no other word for it. In his youth he built his own fiddle and taught himself how to play. He was part of a trio called Cheats & Swings that played for a local square dance troop by the same name. In the 1930s and early 1940s they were thought to be the best in the area. Their reputation was such that they were invited to play for a May Day party that Franklin Roosevelt was giving at Hyde Park. The party was held along the edge of a small pond in which the trio floated in a canoe.

Now, when Walt fiddled he would perch on the edge of his seat and tap both feed, heel and toe. He would also drink. The more he drank the harder he fiddled and the harder he tapped his feet. At one point he kicked a hole in the bottom of the canoe. "It was lucky we capsized when we did or we would have sank for sure," Walt said. Eleanor Roosevelt wrote about Cheats and Swings in her newspaper column but, with her typical grace, left out the part where Uncle Chuck sank the trio in the lily pads.

ISHMAEL, NIXON AND THE FOX

Ishmael smoked and drank for most of his adult life. Even back
in those days this was known to be a bad thing to do. His
supporters and rivals alike warned him that one day he would have
to pay the price. When he was in his 80's he had a stroke and all
those folks who had warned him, at least the few who were not
themselves already dead, said "I told you so".

As a result of the stroke he lost some mobility and had to rely
on a walker or a wheelchair to get around. His mind, which had
always been sharp and mischievous, acquired an intermittent
quality that was both amusing and frustrating.

I had an old VW bus which was most convenient for
transporting Ishmael and his wheelchair. We fashioned a ramp of
plywood so he could be wheeled up and into the side door of the
van. The chair was then held in place with bunji cords which
provided a little excitement but, ultimately, security at the end of
the run. Sometimes we went on trips to the doctor and sometimes
we just went for a ride. Sometimes he remembered who I was and

sometimes he didn't. Once he had me stop by the side of the road near an old, white farmhouse. He told me who had lived there and how he had worked on the house in the days before World War I. "I left my pry bar hanging on a nail between two studs and went to lunch. When I came back the plaster crew had covered it up. Can you go get it, Walt? What do you think?" he implored.

I was certain of two things. First; if I went into the house and punched a hole in the wall where Ishmael directed me to the pry bar would be there. Second; my name was David, not Walt. We left the pry bar hanging.

When it came to politics, Ishmael was one of those independent minded Catskillians who voted for the man, not the party; Hoover, Landon, Willkie, Dewey, Eisenhower, Nixon, Goldwater and then Nixon again. The truth is, by the time the 1970's were ushered in, Ishmael had been trying to vote out Roosevelt for the better part of 40 years. In an uncharacteristic move he had once gone to visit the Roosevelt home at Hyde Park. FDR is buried there and one of the largest blocks of marble ever quarried serves as a marker stone. Only the Tomb of the Unknown Soldier in Arlington sports a bigger slab.

Ishmael stood for a long time and looked at the grave. He then visually surveyed the stone from every angle. "I guess that should hold him," he said.

Needless to say, Ishmael was a big fan of Nixon and was very concerned when it was announced that the President had major tax problems. Tricky Dick had failed to pay taxes on over half a million dollars of income. "I don't understand it," Ishmael said as he shook his head. "How can a man make half a million dollars and not have any money to pay his taxes? Unless, maybe he drinks."

The Watergate hearings vexed my grandfather considerably. He sat in his wheelchair and watched it every day. Like most Americans he found it confusing but, then again, there were days when he found Scooby Doo confusing. Ishmael was convinced that Watergate was a man, a Democrat, and he was out to take Nixon's job. Nixon was a Republican and this was a battle he felt he must fight. Whenever the Democrats seemed to be getting the upper hand he would bang his cane on his walker and swear vengeance on this man Watergate.

There was always plenty of family around and, from time to time, we would try to explain to him that Watergate was not a person but the name of an apartment complex in Washington, DC and that Nixon's problems were bigger than just one man who might be after his job. We never gained any traction and finally just quit trying. In the end, we reasoned, it made little difference if an octogenarian with intermittent dementia understood the ramifications of Watergate or not. When Ishmael would go on his rants about Watergate and just what kind of guy would be trying to take a democratically elected president's job away we would just nod in agreement.

That summer my aunt, Muriel, came for an extended visit. My Uncle Durand, who lived nearby and had been doing his share of home-care for Ishmael, took advantage of the situation and went on vacation.

Muriel was a nurse with many years of experience in dealing with patients who displayed the characteristics that Ishmael was exhibiting. Each day she sat with him in front of the TV and patiently explained, as best she could, what was going on in the hearings. Slowly Ishmael seemed to be getting a grasp of the situation. In time he advanced far enough to be able to ask relevant questions. We were all proud of the work that he and Muriel had been doing.

Things were looking up, for Ishmael if not for Nixon, when Durand returned. He walked into the room where Ishmael was watching TV and sat down.

"What do you think of Watergate?" Ishmael asked.

Durand was unaware of the progress that had been made in his absence. "Sumnabitch is trying to take Nixon's job," was his reply.

"That's what I thought all along," said my grandfather as he looked over at Muriel with betrayal in his eyes.

The look my aunt was giving her brother was somewhat more severe.

The last time I saw Ishmael was early fall. It was southern migratory season and I was packing my van when I got a call from my grandmother, Elfleda. She had seen a rather scruffy-looking fox go into the wood shed. The western red wolf and coyote could be described as "scruffy" even in the most prosperous of times but not so the red fox. A healthy red fox is a thing of beauty, dog show quality beauty. For one to be both scruffy and seen in the daytime - the red fox is nocturnal - was a cause for concern. Rabies was common in the wild and Foxes were not immune. I found a shotgun and some shells and went on down the hill to my grandparents place.

When I arrived, my grandfather was in the driveway heading in the direction of the shed. He had both his walker and wheel chair. The old reprobate was sitting in the chair and wheeling it forward a few feet at a time. He would then reach back to bring the walker up abreast.

I watched for a few minutes, feeling like I was being played. "What are you doing?"

"Fleda saw a fox go into the shed and I'm going to check it out," he said as he spun the chair forward a few feet through the gravel of the drive and then brought the walker up even.

I took the bait. "But why are you taking your walker with you?" I asked.

"It might come after me and I might have to run," he explained.

EPILOGUE – It was a very old fox that had crawled into the shed to die. It lay in the dirt on the floor, its mission accomplished. I put down the gun, picked up a shovel and scooped it into a burlap sack.

On the way out of the shed Ishmael asked to have a look. I held open the sack. The old man looked down at the old fox for quite some time. Foxes and farmers have been enemies almost since the dawn of time. These two ancient warriors may even have done battle over barnyard foul at one time in the past.

"Bury him down by the chicken house," my grandfather said. "He would want it that way."

Note – This story is a bit out of sequence but I thought it a tale worth telling.

THE SUPERBOWL

Starting in the late 1950's and on into the early 1960's football was a game we played out in our piece of overgrown buckwheat field but did not watch very much on television. At that time the only viewing option, on any given Sunday, was the National Football League Giants and they produced a pretty boring product. It seemed as if they were always playing the Bears or Lions in a freezing rain and the end score was 9-6. Things began to change when the American Football League came into existence. This was not your father's brand of football.

My father was a Giants fan and watched religiously every week. When the Giants game finished, usually around 4:30 or 5, the set was free until Ed Sullivan came on in the evening. One Sunday, after the Giants suffered a bitter 6-9 defeat at the hands of the Bears - or maybe it was a 9-6 victory over the Lions - I switched the channel and was amazed at what I saw. It was more football; the Oakland Raiders and the San Diego Chargers playing in Balboa Stadium.

Outside our window the Catskills Mountains were cold and dark but in Balboa Stadium the sun was shining, casting long shadows across the field. The stands were far from full but many of the fans who were there wore sunglasses and short-sleeved shirts. I'd heard about California before and even owned a few Beach Boys 45's but this was the first time the concept of the Golden State was driven home. It was warm and sunny and from my bleak outpost it looked like heaven.

The Raiders had a quarterback named Darrel "The Mad Bomber" Lamonica and the Chargers had a receiver named Lance Alworth. Alworth had a nickname as well, they called him "Bambi", but to my mind a guy named "Lance" had no need for a nickname and shouldn't be taking up a perfectly good one that some other guy could use. In general this new league had much better nicknames than the old NFL. A guy with the nickname of "Bronco" just couldn't hold a candle to the likes of "Gunfighter" Art Powell, "Tombstone" Jackson, "Wahoo" McDaniel, Ron "The Intellectual Assassin" Mix and Elbert "Golden Wheels" Dubenion.

When I tuned in the first half of the game was just coming to a close and the score was 32-27. I was sold. I tried to interest my father in the AFL but he was having none of it. We did not know it at the time but this was the beginning of the generation gap.

The AFL may have been playing an inferior brand of football but it was colorful and exciting. At first they were no match for the NFL but in time, as they got better and better at their liberal game of football, the rivalry between them and the more conservative NFL grew as well. So did the generation gap.

Thing looked to be coming to a head in 1968 when the overachieving New York Jets, led by brash, young, long haired, quarterback, Joe Namath, won the AFL championship. This put them in route to the Orange Bowl in Miami and in the direct path of the juggernaut that was the Baltimore Colts. The Colts were led by Johnny Unitas, he of the flat-topped haircut. The Baltimore team, with their 13-1 record, was considered by many to be the best football team ever assembled. The New York team was considered by many to be prohibitive underdogs.

To give the reader some idea of how long ago this game was played, The field goal kickers approached the ball head-on, the majority of the receivers were white guys and the halftime performers were a collegiate marching band. It might also be useful at this point, in order to set the stage more fully, to review a bit of history. 1968 had been one hell of a year.

The war in Vietnam had been going on for more than half a decade with casualties mounting every year. In January of '68 the Viet Cong launched the Tet Offensive. It was a strategic failure for the VC but a public relations success. Middle-aged men, who once manned the guns during WWII and who now lined the bars in VFW halls across America, were still very much pro-war. But the American fence sitters had been growing less amused by the conflict for quite some time. After Tet they lost their taste for it altogether. War protesting was no longer the domain of fringe elements. Things got ugly. The war would drag on for another seven years but without the hearts and minds of anybody I knew.

April brought the assassination of Martin Luther King. The freedom marches would continue but absent was the grace and dignity he brought to the endeavor.

Robert Kennedy's death in June wiped out any hope that the war would end soon, the generation gap would be bridged and the wounds healed.

In August, Russian tanks rolled into Prague and put out the lights. A similar thing happened at the Democratic Convention when Mayor Richard Daley sent more than 20,000 uniformed thugs into the streets of Chicago to deal with 10,000 peaceful demonstrators. Overkill would be the opposition's weapon of choice.

In November we witnessed the resurrection of Richard Nixon. What good can you say about a man when even his friends don't like him?

As a fitting end to a perfect shit-storm of a year I was selected in December by the members of my community to serve in the armed forces of the United States. For those not up on the lingo of the era, I was drafted. The date I was given to report to Albany was January 13th, 1969.

Jupiter aligns with Mars several times a year and the Moon is in the 7th House for about two hours every day but, as far as I could tell, 1968 just kept getting worse.

The Super Bowl was set for the second Sunday of 1969. For us it wasn't just going to be a game it was going to be a battle of epic proportion; your father's league against yours, pro-war versus anti-war, long hair against short. The 1960's were the most divisive period in American history since the Civil War and this game was shaping up to be a major episode in the story. A sporting event had not packed so much political and social drama since Max Baer, wearing a Star of David on his trunks, fought Hitler's favorite, the German Max Schmeling.

And, as if that weren't enough to stir things up, Spiro "Nolo Contendere" Agnew was in the Colt's locker room before the game giving encouragement to his home-town team. For those readers too young to remember Spiro he was a boodle artist, bagman and former governor of Maryland who rose to the office of vice-president under Nixon. He soon discovered that, by multitasking, he could be both grifter and VP. Agnew was caught raking in the swag in 1973 and entered a no contest plea in court thus gaining his own nickname, "Nolo Contendere". Spiro, the arch enemy of the young, was as polarizing a figure as could be found in 1969. The powder kegs were stacked and the fuses lit.

We all waited for the blast but it never really came. The game itself was a sloppy one and, all in all, rather anti-climatic. It was marked more by fumbles, flubs, interceptions and missed opportunities than by heroics. An ugly game it was but, to my point of view, one with a beautiful result. The Jets prevailed, 16-7, and they did it, ironically, by playing old-time NFL football. Running plays, short passes and field goals dominated and Namath, the man with the rifle for an arm, did not throw a single pass in the fourth quarter.

The game was played on January 12th and the next morning I reported for duty in the United States Army.

MILITARY HISTORY

THE LETTER

The letter did not take me by surprise. Its arrival had been expected for some time. One by one my friends had gotten their letters and one by one I had watched them go. Because of my questionable record in high school, college wasn't an option for me. With nobody to pull strings on my behalf to get me into the reserves or National Guard it was just a matter of time before my turn came.

I didn't have to open the envelope to know what was in it. It didn't have a stamp and the only one I knew who owned their own postal system was my Uncle Sam. Besides, except for my name and address, it was the same as the letters all my friends had been receiving.

"Congratulations," it read, "You have been chosen by the members of your community to serve in the armed forces of the United States."

It sounded like a great honor but the truth was that by 1968 just about every eighteen-year-old without political connections or access to higher education was being drafted. The war in Viet Nam was being fought by conscripts who were mainly poor urban blacks and poor rural whites. My family did not consider themselves poor but we were far from rich. Given other options, I would have turned down the honor of being drafted and settled instead for honorable mention.

The first stop was the induction center in Albany, NY. Here my fellow honorees and I were given the once over before being shuffled off to one fort or another for basic training.

There was a rudimentary IQ test which consisted of 100 multiple choice questions. Each question had four possible answers. In order to qualify for the service you had to score at least 20%. The laws of average dictated that, even if one did not know the answer to any of the questions on the test, a score of 25% was the minimum to be expected. In short, a rhesus monkey with a #2 pencil could score 20% or better. Our inductors reasoned, quite rightly I believe, that if a conscript failed the test it must be a willful act. Anyone scoring less than 20% was believed to have cheated. The bottom line was that anyone who failed the test had their grade automatically rounded up to a passing score. It was my first real-live encounter with Catch 22.

There was a background check that was conducted on the honor system. We were all lined up while an official looking man walked the row and asked each man, "Have you ever been convicted of a felony or misdemeanor of moral turpitude?" The question was an excellent one and most of the future troops gave one of three answers; "Yes", "No" and "What does turpitude mean?" The official looking man carried no pen or clipboard and made no record of the responses.

Next there was a rather primitive physical exam that appeared unchanged since the days of Valley Forge - take a deep breath, stick out your tongue, turn your head and cough. I had polio as a child and, as a result, my left foot was somewhat twisted and a good two sizes smaller than my right. This was not seen as a problem in the Albany induction center but, as the reader will see in future stories, would cause a good deal of head scratching at the Fort Dix reception center.

The last stop before the final swearing in ceremony was a brief mental evaluation. It just wouldn't be right to have people who were mentally unstable going around Southeast Asia committing appalling acts in the name of the United States. Such acts were only meant to be committed by well balanced individuals.

If a conscript wanted to be excused from service on the grounds of being gay, crazy or a conscientious objector this moment with the psychiatrist was their chance to shine. I was quite certain I wasn't gay or crazy but was uncertain as to my feelings about war in general and killing in particular. By the late 60's all but the most

143

patriotically blind knew that Viet Nam was a huge mistake. Without a doubt those of my father's generation who fought against Hitler and Tojo were on a righteous path. To my mind it was quite possible that there could be good wars but Viet Nam was not shaping up to be one. Good war or bad, was it not better to kill than to be killed? I was thinking these things over when my turn in the booth came.

The shrink cut right to the chase. "Do you think you could kill a fellow human being?"

I studied on the questions for a moment and then replied. "Who?"

My interview was over. I was told that I would be given the information as to who was to be killed on a need-to-know basis. The other potential killers and I were hustled through the swearing in ceremony and out onto the sidewalk in front of the building. Two olive drab buses awaited.

The last thing we did before leaving the induction center was to line up and count off by 3s. This was accomplished with some difficulty due to the fact that quite a few of our number had barely broken the 20% barrier on the IQ test. The number 3s were told to take one step forward and then were congratulated for having just become Marines. They got on the lead bus and we never saw them again. The rest of us, the newest members of the United States Army, loaded onto the second bus, the one bound for the pine barrens of New Jersey.

FORT DIX

Like most military installations of its era Fort Dix was built on land suited to little else. The pine barrens of New Jersey do not have much to recommend them beyond the fact that they have long been a dumping ground favored by North Jersey Mafia hit men. The nearby cranberry bogs were ideal for disposing of bodies as well but the acrid waters of the bogs tended to be hard on imported Italian shoes which made the barrens preferable.

The soft, sandy soil of the pine lands, called sugar sand by the locals, made the digging of shallow graves easy work. It also lent itself nicely to fox hole digging. In general, any time you can use the words bogs and barrens to describe a particular stretch of real estate you are talking about an ideal site for a military base.

We got to the fort late that evening and, having not eaten all day, were lucky to find the mess hall still open. Perhaps "lucky" isn't the proper word to be using here. I'd like to describe my first free meal courtesy of the U.S. government but I cannot. It isn't that I don't remember it. The taste remains etched upon my palate and yet, to this day, I have not been able to figure out what that long ago entree was. It may have been tuna roll or cabbage roll or some sort of oversized egg roll. Anyway, it appeared to be something-or-another rolled up or, now that I think of it, it might have curled up of its own volition. It was hard to tell.

The wooden, WWI era barracks of the reception center would be, in theory, our home for the next 3-4 days after which we would move on to basic training. Each morning we awoke and marched off for haircuts, shots, testing, or instructional lectures. Some of these events took place in a series of long, low, temporary structures but much of the in-processing revolved around a large, oddly shaped building that stood about a quarter of a mile from the barracks. It was called Central Depot.

Both physical and mental testing was carried out in this building and most of it was fairly basic. One day we took a long protracted aptitude test. There were hundreds of simple and seemingly harmless questions. Do you make friends easily? Would you rather drive a car or ride in one? Every once in a while they threw in a ringer. Can you go a long time without water? Can you find your way well in the woods?

Now I grew up in the woods and always found my way home and I suppose I can go as long without water as the next guy but saw no reason to share this information with the Army. From my point of view being left in the woods without water was a situation to be avoided. My answer to both of those questions and to the other ones like them was No.

I believe these were necessary precautions that I took but it was neither during aptitude testing nor even at Central Depot that my future was determined, at least not yet. It was in one of the outlying structures, at the far end of the uniform line, the end where we were to be fitted with boots, that fate stepped in.

To understand what happened to me next one must understand a little about the Army. It is often said that there are three ways of doing things – the right way, the wrong way and the Army way. As odd as it may seem, the United States Army is not part of the United States. It exists as its own separate fiefdom; a country within a country. It has its own manner of dress, its own language, customs, food, legal system and, most of all, rules.

Rules govern every aspect of Army life from the tilt of your hat to the shine on your shoes. And the shine is not the only part of military footwear that is regulated. There is, for example, a rule that says a recruit cannot be issued a shoe smaller than his foot. Another rule forbids the issuance of a shoe that is more than one size larger than a recruit's foot. As I may have mentioned earlier, a childhood encounter with polio left me with mismatched feet; one size 10 and one 8. When it came my turn to be measured for and issued boots the war effort ground to a halt.

The man doing the measuring shook his head and then dutifully wrote down the two different shoe sizes in the appropriate boxes of the Department of Defense form. He passed the form along to the man behind the counter.

The counter man looked to be retired military; most of the people who worked in the uniform barn were. This gentleman appeared to be retired Marine Corps judging by his haircut and tattoos. He stared at the DOD form for quite some time and then turned to look at the endless rows of shelves filled with matched pairs for shiny black boots. He placed the form on the counter in front of him and, cradling his head with both hands, studied on the problem. It was obvious that handing out boots was near the upper limits of his capabilities and this development was pushing him over the top. "10's is too big and 8's is too small. I'm not sure what to do about this."

I must confess I was feeling rather proud of myself having created my own Catch 22 after only 2 days in the Army but the pained look on the face of the old Marine was cause for concern. He seemed to be asking me for help and a part of me felt bad about causing him such distress.

"How about just breaking up a pair," I offered. "Give me one size 10 and one size 8. You got plenty of boots. Whose gunna know?"

The old jarhead looked at me like I had just suggested that he and I go out to Liberty Island and relieve ourselves on the statue lady's sandals. "I better call my supervisor," he said.

The supervisor looked to be, if anything, even more retired. He and the counter man put their heads together and then called for reinforcements. The gathering was beginning to resemble a rugby scrum. After considerable discussion they broke the huddle and the senior member, a portly gentleman who seemed to be extremely retired and a bit resentful of my intrusion into the tranquility of his golden years, handed me the offending form. "We can only break up a pair of boots with written permission from a doctor."

"A doctor?" I said, never at loss for words.

"You have to go out to Walson," he explained as he filled out a routing slip to the base hospital. "Go out the door behind you and turn right. Walk about a quarter of a mile and you will see it."

I could hear a collective sigh of relief as I left.

Walson Army Hospital, bright and modern, stood not far from, but in sharp contrast to, the Doughboy era reception center. It was not hard to find and I soon located a doctor who looked at my feet and signed my shoe request. He was a bit concerned that the rigors of basic training might cause me discomfort. This took me by surprise. I had assumed that the rigors of basic training were designed primarily to cause discomfort but accepted the limited duty slip, good for 60 days, which he offered to me.

"That should hold you through basic. Come back if you are having any trouble after the 60 days runs out and I'll give you another 60," he explained. "And if you haven't had lunch I suggest you eat here at the hospital before going back to the reception center."

His advice was good. In the Bizarro world of the Army the best food was hospital food.

Back at the building that served as headquarters for the reception center the sergeant behind the desk read over my limited duty slip and shook his head. "They aren't going to like this over at basic. No running, jumping, prolonged walking or standing; my God, that's all they ever do in basic training. They aren't going to like this one bit. They will just send you right back here and tell us to keep you for 60 days until your condition improves."

"It's more or less a permanent condition," I tried to explain. "My left foot has been smaller than the right for as long as I can remember; ten, maybe fifteen years or more. It's not likely to grow a size a month for the next two months."

The sergeant turned the paper around so I could see it and ran his finger under the words at the top. "See this here? It says 'Temporary Limited Duty'. What you have is a temporary condition." He shifted his finger to the bottom of the page. "Now see this here? This is not just the signature of a doctor it is the signature of an officer in the United States Army."

I wasn't sure of the point he was trying to make and, quite frankly, I don't think he was either.

"We'll put you in the medical hold barracks for 60 days and then you will report back to the hospital. If your condition hasn't improved any by the end of 60 days that doctor will decide what to do with you next," the desk sergeant said as he dismissed me.

Basic training would not take me while I had a limited duty slip and the doctor at Walson indicated that he would be willing to give me as many limited duty slips as it took to get me through basic training. This was my second Catch 22 in the same day. Despite all my misgivings I was certainly beginning to show a real flair for military life.

Medical hold was a menagerie, a gathering of misfits, a Salon des Refusés. The military, it seems, had no control over the draft board other than to tell them the number of warm bodies that were required. By the late 1960's volunteers were scarce and even the Selective Service was nearing the bottom of the barrel. In order to make their numbers the draft board was sending people that the military had no use for; people with, among other peculiarities, ruptured discs, uncorrectable vision problems such as legal blindness and irregularities of the heart.

Having been sworn into the Army at various induction centers around the northeast these people were sent to Fort Dix where they were culled from the system. There was a story about a conscript who had a glass eye. Upon failing the preliminary eye exam the doctor asked him if there was something wrong with his one eye. The conscript removed the glass eye, looked it over with the good one and said "Nope". This may have only been a story but it's a good one and, to anybody who served in the Army in the late sixties, a believable one as well.

All these unwanted souls were gathered together in the medical hold barracks at the reception center of the fort. It took but a moment at the induction centers around the area to swear them in but the out-processing took three weeks or more. There was no explanation for this that I could ever find other than this was the "Army Way". It was into this mix that I was dropped to spend the next 60 days doing my best to grow my left foot another two sizes.

The Medical Hold barracks was capable of holding as many as forty men but it was little more than half full. Most of the occupants were eighteen or nineteen years old and some were younger. Some had been there just a few days while others were nearing the end of their three week stay. Sometimes they talked about what they did before they were drafted into the Army. In the summer of 1969 the Draft Board eliminated educational deferments and all the college kids were funneled into the service but this was January and the kids in medical hold at that time were, for one reason or another, just not college material. Mostly they worked in manual labor or the service industries. Lester, for example, worked on a dock someplace in Connecticut. The dock mainly served sport fishing boats. It was his job to chop up the fish for chum used to bait the waters. Randall was a pimp in Trenton, New Jersey.

Sometimes the inmates talked about what they were going to do after they got out of the Army. Generally it was the same thing as they did before. Lester would go back to chopping up dead fish and Randall would go back to tending his own fleet. Sometimes they talked of other things but mostly they talked of paperwork. Which papers they already had and which papers they needed to get; which offices were notoriously slow and which file clerks could be useful. Having accepted these troopers, sight unseen, the Army was now responsible for them and wanted to make sure they were discharged in the proper fashion. A lot of paperwork was needed to accomplish that.

We were not completely in the Army and we were not out. We were dressed like soldiers and looked like soldiers so we decided to act, as best we could, like soldiers. In the Army, when two men have the same rank, the leadership role goes to the one with the most time in grade. In our world of limbo we were all buck privates but "One Lung" Lepkowski, who had been in the Army for over a month, had been a buck private the longest. He was the nominal leader. Second in command was "Big Red".

One Lung actually had two functioning lungs. He got his name when one of them collapsed during the second day of in-processing. It had happened while he was trying to run and carry a duffel bag that was nearly as big as he was. They had re-inflated the lung out at the hospital and were now waiting six weeks or so to see if the patch held.

Big Red came by his name honestly. He was six feet three and weighed nearly 300 pounds with very red hair. When he first showed up at the reception center he weighed about 275 and very little of it was muscle. It was decided that his weight could constitute a health hazard in basic training so he had been assigned to medical hold, given weight-loss pills and put on a strict diet.

When Big Red went through the chow line he had to wear a sign that said "Fat Boy". The servers gave him only salad. Despite the Army's best intentions Big Red had gained nearly 25 pounds in a little over three weeks. This is the kind of production that they look for from cattle in a west Texas feeder lot. It was, however, not what the Army was looking for.

Big Red might have had to survive his days on leafy green vegetables but night time was a different story. After dark the other members of medical hold would sneak out to the roach coach that parked near the hospital and bring back hero sandwiches, bags of chips and pints of ice cream for him. The roach coach would not sell directly to Big Red (his picture was taped to the side of the van) but the big man tipped his couriers generously with diet pills so he was never in want.

My 60 day sentence was extremely long by Medical Hold standards. In time One Lung recovered enough to be sent on to basic. Shortly after that the Army got tired of supporting Big Red's Ramadan of fasting all day and feasting all night and sent him packing for home. With the two of them gone I became the nominal leader, the King Rat of Medical Hold. In spite of the fact that the position carried no duties or responsibilities I believe I handled it with dignity.

MICHELANGELO OF THE PINE BARRENS

All members of Medical Hold were assigned a day job during their short stay. As much as possible the jobs were matched to their capabilities. Some picked up litter around the compound while others worked in the mess hall or stocked shelves in the uniform barn. Big Red, being a senior member of the tribe, got to answer the phone in the HQ building. He was proud of the fact that the old, wooden office chair had to be reinforced with two sections of angle iron from the motor pool. One Lung Lepkowski, our leader, disappeared every day after breakfast and didn't reappear until dinner in the evening. I never knew where Lung spent his days and I don't believe anybody else did either. My stay was to be a long one by Medical Hold standards so I was given a routing slip and told to report to the Sergeant Major at the Central Depot for an assignment.

As mentioned before, Central Depot was a large building and somewhat separated from the living area of the newly arrived troops. It was used for testing of all sorts and anything else that troops could be lined up to do. It also provided office space for the command. The structure was built in the shape of a cross, like a

Gothic Cathedral with long transepts and a nave on the end. The center atrium was a story and a half high with a clerestory for illumination. It is important to keep in mind here that in the face of flowery language, the use of words like atrium, transept and clerestory, this Central Depot was built at the start of WWI as a mule barn. In spite of numerous renovations it had never been able to entirely outdistance its past. The smell of mule, which was the reason for the building being located a quarter mile downwind of the billeting area, was long gone but the ambiance remained.

The atrium was large and barren. There was a double door that led down each wing and the rest was blank walls punctuated by the occasional small bulletin board or 8"x10" photo of a general or politician. When the weather was bad the conscripts would stand in a line against the walls and wait for their turn at one test or another. There were a few folding chairs tucked under a Formica topped table on one side of the space but nothing else.

Upon my arrival I was instructed to sit in one of the chairs to await the Sergeant Major. I'd been in the atrium before but only passing through as part of the herd. My previous visits had been fleeting and I hadn't noticed the beginnings of a pencil sketch on a portion of one of the walls. On the table was a print of a painting entitled *Remagen Bridgehead Assault*. It was a lively picture of gung-ho WWII era GIs charging into battle; lots of guns, jeeps and

162

tanks. The pencil sketch, the part that was complete, was done from the print. It was stiff and labored. There was another more subtle problem, the print was sized on a 2-to-3 ratio; 20 inches high by 30 inches long. The wall section, above the wainscot and below the clerestory, was more on the scale of 1-to-3; 5 feet high by 15 feet long. Obviously the painting could be enlarged using a one-to-one ratio but the end product would not fit the intended space. It would have to be elongated by adding figures, implements of destruction and landscaping.

I found a pencil on the table next to the print and began to make a sketch on the back of my routing slip. The sky was easy to expand. I brought in some of the aircraft from my day of plane spotting in the Catskills Mountains and whipped them into a dogfight. More soldiers of the 9th armored division were called from the wings and more armored vehicles wheeled in as well. The battle raged as skies darkened and smoke from a burning tank rolled across the field. Completely lost in the action it was as if I were, once again, back in Miss Olin's sixth grade class.

Reality intruded when the Sergeant Major cleared his throat and brought me back from the 1940's to the 1960's. "Step into my office," he ordered. He was a stout man in his 60's and looked, in my opinion, a little like Miss Olin around the eyes.

In his office I was invited to sit while he looked over my routing slip both front and back. "This is an official military document," he said as he focused on the back.

I began a string of humble apologies but he waved them off. "So it looks like you have been to art school."

"Yes sir," I said, sensing an opportunity. "Two years."

"Where did you go?" he asked.

The answer to this question was critical. I had to come up with an art school and it had to be one the Sergeant Major was not familiar with. He didn't seem to be the type of person who would know much about the world of academic art, or art at all for that matter, but I was sitting there without as much as a picture card in my hand. If he called my bluff it was all over. Not only had I never gone to art school but high school art classes were missing from my resume as well. I couldn't afford follow-up questions from the old soldier. I had to come up with an answer and my choices were limited, extremely limited in fact. Pratt Institute in Brooklyn was the only art school I had ever heard of.

"Pratt." I said with conviction.

Bingo. I spent the remainder of my 60-day limited duty slip painting murals in the atrium at Central Depot. When that slip ran out the doctor, who seemed to enjoy butting heads with the Army, gave me another 60 days and, after that one ran out, a 90 day slip. I was in position to spend my 2-year tour of duty painting murals in New Jersey and, to the best of my knowledge, nobody had ever gotten shot while painting a mural at Fort Dix.

And I would have spent my entire military career ensconced in my own little Sistine Chapel but I got lazy and bored. Lazy and bored, in and of themselves, are not the kind of things that raise red flags in the Army but I went beyond that. I got irreverent and careless.

GOD'S OWN HANGOVER

The denizens of the Medical Hold Barracks were a merry lot and well they should be. Just weeks, if not days, before they were being rounded up from places likes Hartford, Connecticut, Appleton, Maine, Dover Delaware, Aurora, New York and Trenton, New Jersey. They had been processed and shipped to Fort Dix with what may have seemed like a death sentence hanging over their heads. Each man had said goodbye to his friends, made peace with his Gods and enemies and steeled himself to face the rigors of basic training and, quite possibly, the horrors of jungle warfare. And then out of nowhere, like an eleventh-hour, death row call from the Governor, they had gotten word that they were being set free.

These men were primed to party at the drop of a hat and so when legitimate occasions arose there was no holding them back. Big Red's departure, after more than two months in Medical Hold, was just such an occasion. The big man was leaving on Monday so Saturday night was chosen for the bon voyage celebration.

Just outside the main gate was a liquor store that stocked an excellent selection of wines catering to our tastes. They had Bali Hi, Ripple in traditional Red as well as Pagan Pink and the hard-to-find Pear, MD 20/20 which was known affectingly as Mad Dog, Night Train and Wild Irish Rose AKA Wild Eye. But for economy and shear stopping power you couldn't beat Thunderbird. It also had a catchy jingle that went along with it; What's the word? / Thunderbird / How's it sold? / Good and cold / What's the jive? / Bird's alive / What's the price? / 44 twice. For less than a dollar you could get a bottle of Thunderbird and that included the tax and a paper bag. The cheap, fortified wine complimented the Darvon capsules that were so prevalent. In honor of the occasion Big Red broke out the last of his diet pills.

Recruits were not permitted radios in the Reception Center but somehow we had one. *The Who* had just released their rock opera, *Tommy*, and an avant garde radio station in Philadelphia was going to play all four sides of the double album without interruption starting at 10 that night. We drank wine, popped pills, played crazy eights, listened to The Who and ate junk food from the roach coach until wee hours.

Thunderbird is a foul tasting fruit of the vine which, like Texas water, should not be taken internally. If either must be drunk they should be drunk as cold as possible. When quaffed at room

168

temperature T-bird cut like a razor. We had no ice or refrigeration. It was only by raw courage and sheer determination that we were able to get it down, at least at first. Things got easier as the evening wore on. T-bird, known as the Campbell's Soup of cheap wine, can be very unpredictable especially when mixed with diet pills and Darvon. Some threw up, some passed out and some did both. Big Red became very melancholy as he looked back over his military career and began to cry. Several other detainees cried with him.

Robertson, a plumber's assistant from western Massachusetts, got the idea that he could use one of his bed sheets as a parachute by holding the four corners, two in each hand. Extending off the back of the barracks was a small balcony and a set of wooden stairs that served as a fire escape. Robinson's plan was to use this space as a testing ground for his hypothesis. Disregarding the fact that the bed sheet/parachute theory had been disproved countless times by Wiley Coyote, he climbed up on the railing and jumped.

Considering all of this with the benefit of hindsight it is clear to see that we should have done more to try and talk him out of it but, truth be told, at the time it was the majority opinion of Robertson's peers that it would work. As for myself, I was soon to be the leader of the band and was looking forward to expanding my prestige if not my power by adding a Medical Hold airborne division. Fortunately, one of the small cedar trees common to the area broke his fall. Unfortunately it also broke Robertson's collar bone and left wrist.

There was a rumor that Thunderbird contained more than a trace of formaldehyde. This might have been only a rumor but I awoke the next morning feeling ready for the slab. My head could not be moved without pain. Indeed, it was painful even to try to move my eyes. I tried to raise my head but my neck could not hold its burden. My skull fell back onto the pillow like a bowling ball and the ripple of the bed springs caused my stomach to churn. I could turn my head neither left nor right and a sense of panic overcame me. If I were to vomit in this position it would surely result in death by drowning.

A task force was being assembled to transport Robertson to the hospital and I pleaded to be taken along. Even on Sunday the Medical Hold barracks wasn't a restful place to be. It was never a good idea to be found lying in your bunk during the daytime. I needed a slip from a health care professional entitling me to twenty-four hour bed rest.

At the hospital the medic looked in my ears and down my throat and then felt the glands in my neck. I winced with pain with his every move. I really needed that bed rest and so when he put the thermometer in my mouth and turned away I ran my tongue back and forth over the bulb to create some friction and bring the temperature up.

The medic got distracted and was late returning for the thermometer. By then I had run the temperature up fairly high. He told me that a recruit at Fort Dix had recently died of spinal meningitis. He was uncertain as to whether or not I had that particular disease but he was taking no chances. He was going to admit me to the hospital and let the doctors decide. At this point it might have been a good idea for me to admit that my condition was the result of staying up most of the night drinking bum wine but this guy looked to be a bit of a prig. I was afraid he would send me back to Medical Hold without so much as an APC*.

"Do you think that's necessary?" I asked.

"I'm sending you down to the lab for blood work and then I'll schedule an enema to clean you out good for x-ray," the medic said and he scribbled on a pad in front of him on the desk.

"Alright," I said in resignation. "We were up drinking last night and I have a hangover. That's all it is, just a hangover.

"What's the word?" he sang as he handed me a slip for twenty-four bed rest and a generous hand-full of APCs.

"Thunderbird," I conceded.

171

*APC – All Purpose Capsule containing aspirin, butalbital, caffeine and phenacetin. Some were rumored to contain codeine and were highly prized. After all, this was the 1960's. Not to be confused with APC – Armored Personnel Carrier.

THE HULK

Painting a mural was, at first, a glorious thing to be doing and I considered myself the luckiest man in the Army, that is, if I was truly in the Army. There was still some question as to whether or not I was but those questions did not concern me.

Art supplies had to be found. Pencils were plentiful and the back reaches of a supply room produced a roll of brown butcher paper that must have been there from the days when the structure was a mule barn. What connected Army Mules and butcher paper was a question better left unasked. I rolled out enough to reproduce the wall section but in a smaller scale, flattened it as much as possible and began to sketch.

The hobby section of the base PX provided paint and brushes while a clip board drilled with a thumb hole passed easily for a pallet. The brushes were small as was the pallet and it was a big wall but that fit my plan to a T. I could take many months to cover 125 square feet of wall surface with a number 2 brush. The chairs stacked on the table served as scaffolding to reach the top sections and, with a little practice, I was able to jump from one chair to the next with pallet in hand.

At first it was exhilarating, like running down the beach and into the ocean on a warm summer's day. But, like running into the ocean, the farther in I got the more effort it required just to keep going. It wasn't that there was no positive feedback, every officer and non-commissioned officer who passed through the atrium commented on how well the mural was proceeding. The conscripts who often lined the walls enjoyed the work as well. My problem was that I never had a job before; at least not one that required me to be in the same place doing the same thing every day. It began to gnaw on me.

By the time I started on my second 60 days of limited duty I was spending as much time talking with the inductees as painting. Like me, the overwhelming majority of them had been drafted. Some were actual volunteers but most of the ones who had enlisted did so because they had been led by an unscrupulous recruiter to believe they would get a better deal. None were enthralled with the proceedings in general but the mural in progress broke the monotony and provided a welcome distraction.

When I got my third limited duty slip, this one for 90 days, it was beginning to feel more like a prison sentence than a blessing. I took to arriving for work late, goofing off a lot during the day and quitting early. This kind of behavior was not out of the ordinary in the military at the time and would have gone unnoticed for months if not years but I took my disrespect for the establishment a step farther.

My problems began when one of the conscripts pointed out to me that the hub of the front wheel of a half track looked like a peace sign. I decided to go with it. A week later the steering wheel of a jeep, which should have taken the shape of a Mercedes logo, became a peace symbol as well. I thought that to be rather clever and, in as much as it was partially obscured by the drivers arm, undetectable by the casual viewer. By August there were dozens of peace symbols hidden, to some degree or another, in the painting. I even went so far as to have one of the attacking troopers flashing fingers in the form of a V.

One morning I arrived for work, late as was my custom, only to find the Sergeant Major and Executive Officer standing in front of my work. The XO, second in command, was a man with the build and mustache of Oliver Hardy and the nose of W.C. Fields. His expression always made him look like he might have a dill pickle spear lodged in his throat. It had taken him nearly twenty years to rise to the rank of Captain. He was going no higher and everybody knew it. The XO started drinking everyday during lunch and kept it up throughout the afternoon and everybody knew that as well. His office always smelled heavily of cigarettes and breath mints.

The jig was up. They made me paint out all the peace symbols, at least all they could find. I even went so far as to paint out one or two that they had missed although I'm sure some were missed by all. My humiliation was carried out in front of an extended line of conscripts who all watched with amusement. For me it was Miss Olin's class all over again. When my reprimand was complete the First Sergeant turned to go but the XO held his ground.

The officer in charge of Central Depot was on medical leave and this was the XO's moment in the sun. "This kind of insubordination will not go unpunished on my watch."

The First Sergeant was under the impression that the insubordination had been punished but he was a survivor who knew when to fight and when to retreat. He had little use for the XO but in this case retreat was the smart move.

The XO walked over to the line of recruits and selected the largest one he could find. He led the mystified inductee over next to me. The XO looked at the man's name tag, looked once again and then said to me. "Hulk will escort you back to the Medical Hold barracks where you will remain under house arrest until I call for you."

It was a common thing in the army to give a man an instant nickname based on physical characteristics; Big Red was an excellent example of that process in action. Sometimes the nickname came about because the person's real name was too hard to pronounce; Jannicki might become Jinks, Mangionelli might become Mango. Huldenbeck, my recently deputized escort, met both criteria. Not only did his name have more than two syllables but he was an imposing presence.

One of the hardest things to come to terms with as a person makes the adjustment from civilian to military life is the inability to size up his peers by how they look. The old saw, "You can't judge a book by its cover", is not entirely true. We form our first impressions of a person by how they dress and wear their hair and, as often as not, those impressions are accurate. The first thing the Army does is to shave all the heads and dress all the bodies in identical green outfits. Hulk could have been a hit man from Staten Island or a lowly motor vehicle clerk from Yonkers.

The only thing I could tell about my watch dog was that his newly sheared dome revealed a number of scars. He also seemed to be a bit older than the average conscript; mid-twenties or so. In the late 1960's the fact that a man had done time in prison didn't prevent him from being drafted upon his release. I accepted the possibility that Hulk was a former inmate. There had been several ex-cons passing through Medical Hold. They were a fairly well behaved lot and knew, to the man, how to operate a floor buffer. I would have to watch my step with Hulk.

With an air of ceremony The XO removed the pencils and paintbrushes from my shirt pocket. He lined us up; me in front and Hulk in the back. "Forward harch," he barked and then, although it was not yet 10:30, retreated into his office for a nip.

THE HULK PART 2

HOUSE ARREST

On our way from Central Depot to the Medical Hold barracks I tried to take the measure of Hulk, my own private jailer.

"What's your real name? I mean, what name do you go by?" I asked back over my shoulder.

"Butch," was his reply.

From my point of view, Butch didn't seem to be much of an improvement. "Would you prefer Butch over Hulk?"

"Vastly," he said.

He had only spoken two words and yet my feeling was that here was a man I could deal with. I fell back and walked at his side. "Look, neither one of us has any experience with house arrest. Let's just keep a low profile and things will be fine," I said. "Do you know where Medical Hold is?"

Butch did not. I explained its location and suggested we stop by and collect his gear on the way.

"The XO will be doing some light drinking the rest of the day. He keeps his own counsel while that is going on so you can forget about the inquest being today. The high gear drinking starts as soon as he gets off work. Today is Friday so we're not going to hear from him until Monday at the earliest and your group is shipping out to basic this afternoon," I said.

Butch stopped in his tracks and looked down at me. "How do you know this?"

"You've seen the man. He has a snout as red as a stoplight," I said.

"Not that part," Butch replied. "How do you know my group is shipping to basic today? They never told us anything about it."

"Elementary, Watson. The pink glow is gone from your scalp. Your head was shaved at least three days ago. The line you were in was for Psychological Profile which, along with Auditory Discrimination testing, is just about the last thing you do here in the reception station. It rained last night and when it does the area around the Auditory Discrimination building turns into a quagmire. There is no mud on your boots so you haven't been there already. My guess is that your group is going to AD right after Psyche Profile and then it's off to basic." I said. "And, by the way, they never do tell you anything."

Butch and I gathered his gear from his quarters and set up a bunk for him in Medical Hold. Several members of our fraternity were hanging around, getting ready to report to the mess hall to be servers for lunch. Exercising my rights as leader of the pack I asked them to bring us back two lunches. It was a beautiful day after the rain and we ate on the steps at the back of the barracks. I filled him in, to the best of my knowledge, on the workings of Medical Hold, the Reception Center and the Army in general. Mostly it was just basic information every recruit is eager to know. He asked a few questions about my situation and I was beginning to get the feeling that he might not be an ex-con after all.

After we finished lunch Butch asked me if there was a library on post. There was a barracks that combined both library and day-room. We walked over that way. The library was on the ground floor. Butch looked around and then walked to a shelf that held a row of seemingly identical volumes. He took one down and sat at one of the tables in the center of the room. I took the seat across from him.

"UMCJ," he said. "Universal Code of Military Justice; It's what they call the law here in the army. Ironically, we, the protectors of the Constitution, are not covered by it. The UMCJ is universal, military and a code so it has very little to do with justice but it's what we have so let's see if it can work for us."

"What did you do on the outside?" I asked Butch.

"I was an attorney," he said as he returned that volume and selected another from down along the row. "Give me a dollar and I'll be yours."

I was happy to ante up. Butch spent about two hours reading through sections of the books, asking me questions and making notes with a stump of a pencil on the small scraps of paper the library provided.

On the way out I suggested we go upstairs to the day room. The day-room was poorly named as it was not much fun during the day. It had a sagging pool table, a ping pong table without a net and a television that only got stations from Philadelphia during the daytime. Corporal Paff, the NCO in charge, had a thick Eastern European accent and could be a genuine prick toward Medical Hold personnel who he didn't consider real soldiers. He called me Private Russ and said it as if my claim to the title of Private was questionable. I usually avoided the place during daylight hours but I wanted to check the latch on the storeroom window.

After dinner Butch and I hung out, playing cards with my minions, my knights of the round table. They were, to a man, duly impressed that I was under house arrest and had my own body guard. Butch proved to be very good at cards which made me wonder if he had, in reality, practiced only jailhouse law.

At 7:00 PM the day-room closed and Butch and I headed over that way. The television antenna at the back of the day-room gave easy access to the storeroom window. It had taken me a while to discover this access route and I chose not to share it with the rest of the Medical Holds. They were a transient lot and prone to flamboyancy. It was important that my sanctuary remain undetected.

We got quickly inside, pulled down the World War II blackout blinds and turned on the TV. At night the New York stations came in. The Mets were playing, Seaver was pitching and all was well with the world.

From time to time the announcers would pass on reports that they were getting from other sources. There was something going on in upstate New York. A music festival of sorts seemed to be growing out of control. Tens of thousands, maybe even hundreds of thousands of kids were being drawn to the mountains. The roads were clogged, the New York Thruway closed. Although circumstances prevented us from attending the Woodstock

Festival, Three days of Peace and Music, was a powerful moment for us. It was being held 150 miles to the north but we were empowered by it.

At 0900 hours on Monday morning the XO summoned us to his office. The First Sergeant was present as was a scribe with a crisp new legal pad. The scribes scalp was glowing a rosy pink.

"You can wait outside, Hulk," the XO said.

Butch came to attention, "Private Rose is entitled to council and I am here in that capacity. We would like to know the charges against my client."

The XO was stunned and nervously looked down at his desk drawer, the one where he kept the bottle.

The First Sergeant was a thoroughly decent man who had too much respect for the Army to have any respect at all for the XO. He tried not to laugh as he read the charge. "Insubordination."

Butch took the clipped notes from his pocket and flipped through them. "Is it your contention that Private Rose disobeyed direct orders as to what to paint and what not to paint in the mural?"

"He should have known better," the XO blustered but it was clear he was now on the defense. "He painted peace symbols."

Butch pressed the advantage. "Do you have any copies of written orders or witnesses to verbal ones forbidding him to paint such symbols?"

The XO crossed out something on the paper in front of him and began to write in something else.

Butch leaned over to see what he was doing. "I needn't remind you that the document before you is a legal one and that the charges against my client cannot be amended at this point."

The XO threw down his pen, grabbed his hat from the hook on the wall and stalked out of the office.

The First Sergeant smiled as he filled out the routing slips. "Rose, take Huldenbeck over to Psyche Profile and AR and then go gather your gear. You two are going to basic.

On our way to gather our gear I told Butch that I thought he was a pretty good lawyer. "Too good to get drafted into the Army," I added.

"You're right on that point," Butch said. "I enlisted."

As it turned out, Butch's younger brother had been drafted, sent to Viet Nam and killed in action. The Hulk was in the Army to get even.

SALTY DOG AND THE NUTLEY PECKER-HEAD

After basic training I was schooled as a welder and then sent overseas to Okinawa. The flight was a long one, made longer yet by my seatmate on that military transport. I have long ago forgotten his name but he was from Nutley, New Jersey. This annoying little pecker-head spent the entire flight telling me the stories of his life. Nutley was 19, the same age as me, so there wasn't a lot of life to his stories. Mostly his tales were about hanging out with his high school buddies, drinking, drinking and driving and doing mean-spirited things to people who were not like them. These misdeeds were almost always done while drinking and driving.

I looked forward to parting ways with Nutley when we landed in Okinawa but, as fate directed, that was not to be. Not only was he assigned to the same company as me but the same platoon, same squad and to the very bunk beneath mine. It was beginning to look like I would be Nutley's companion for the duration.

On Saturday night, in the second week of our exile, Nutley came to me, his new best friend, and asked to borrow five dollars.

That was a princely sum on the island of Okinawa in the 1960's. It represented about half of my net worth but, for some unexplainable reason, I gave him the money.

The little twerp was going down to Naha City to kick up his heels. He asked me if I wanted to go and even offered to buy me a drink with my very own fiver. I declined.

It was no surprise to find, upon awakening Sunday morning, Nutley had not yet returned. It should be understood that Okinawa was not unlike Pleasure Island in Pinocchio. Substitute thousands of loosely supervised teenagers for young boys and drugs and alcohol for ice cream and candy. Apparently Nutley had set right to work growing his donkey ears and tail. Five dollars, if spent prudently in the Nominoui section of Naha, could leave a man as dried up as a sun-bleached dog turd on a summer sidewalk.

By Sunday evening Nutley's absence was beginning to be noticed and when he failed to appear for formation on Monday morning there was much speculation as to his fate. Okinawa, affectionately referred as "The Rock", was a small island in the middle of the East China Sea. There was really no place for Nutley to go. On Tuesday the MPs showed up with bolt cutters, snipped the lock from his foot locker and, without ceremony, stuffed his belongings into his duffel bag.

I never saw the Nutley pecker-head again. Needless to say, I never saw my five dollars again either. I have always considered it to be money well spent.

Ironically, Nutley's replacement was from New Jersey as well, from Tom's River. His name has also been lost to history but that is of little consequence as it was never used in the barracks. We all just called him Salty Dog.

I must say, the man was as fine a doper as I have ever known. With him there was none of the denial, misdirection, and duplicity that is so unappealing in drug addicts and alcoholics. He did not brag about who he was but he did not run from it either.

The Army of the late 1960's was much different than the one we know today. Volunteers were few and far between and even conscripts were getting hard to find. In order to fill the ranks, the military and the justice department joined together and came up with a unique program. Certain civilian offenders, upon being found guilty by the courts, were given a choice by the judge, three years in the Army or five years in jail. Almost all of them took the military option. While some of these offenders were real criminals who should have been in jail a lot of them were just kids who got nailed for simple possession of marijuana. This transgression, while considered minor today, carried stiff penalties at that time.

Salty Dog was a three-or-five man but not a criminal by any modern standards. His only aspirations were to do his time, get high whenever he could and get back to his Harley Sportster in Toms River. This is not to say that he would not, from time to time, steal my radio or box fan to sell for drug money. But, to his credit, he only did these things when nearing the end of a drug binge and always felt genuine remorse for his actions.

When measured by the mind altering standards of Americans in the 1960s the Okinawans were primitive people. They had no concept of recreational drug use. Many pharmaceuticals that were considered controlled substances in the States were available over the counter in an Okinawan drug store. The indigenous people would never think to purchase and ingest a drug they did not need. However, possession of some drugs was illegal on the island. These illegal substances were slightly harder to obtain, at least during daylight hours.

Faced with a virtual smorgasbord of uppers and downers Salty Dog was in heaven. He tried it all but settled, oddly enough, on huffing model airplane glue. He first experimented with glue during those lean days before the end of the month when we were all economizing, trying to stretch each dollar until payday. Glue was only meant to be a stopgap measure but somehow it became a standard in Salty Dog's repertoire.

Even in those by-gone days, the dangers of inhaling glues and solvents were well known. I explained to my friend the downside of his hobby, how it could bring on permanent brain damage by eating holes in the gray matter. Salty Dog was not to be deterred. "If you do other drugs, and get the balance just right, you start seeing things," he explained. "You may say to yourself, 'Hey man, I'm hallucinating'. When you sniff glue you don't hallucinate, those suckers are real."

Shortly after our talk I was awakened in the dead of night by the sounds of panic and distress. Salty Dog was out of his bed and sitting on the floor, his back up against a wall locker. He was out of breath and sweating profusely. From his position he could lean out and look down the aisle that transected the barracks. He did so and what he saw terrified him. "It's after me," he said breathlessly. "It chased me from the motor pool and now it's here. You have to stop it, I can't run anymore."

"Tell me, Salty Dog, what is it?" I said as jumped down from my bed and retrieved the bunk adapter – a two-foot section of metal pipe – I kept beneath the edge of my mattress.

"It's a whale!"

THE ROCK

In the spring and early summer of 1945 Okinawa, the principal island in the Ryukyu chain, was the deadliest place on earth. Little more than a glorified atoll, 60 miles long by 15 miles wide, it saw a quarter of a million people die as the American Army, Navy and Marines tried to wrest the island from Japanese control. Twice as many sailors died here as were lost during the attack on Pearl Harbor. 1,500 Kamikazes accounted for most of the Navy losses at Okinawa.

By the time I landed, twenty-five years later, things had quieted down considerably. While almost all Okinawans agreed that the Americans were more easily tolerated than the Japanese Imperial Forces they replaced the islanders were not entirely comfortable with our military presence. The Navy at Naha, Marines at Futenma, and Army at Machinato offered their own unique problems but it was the air base at Kedena that seemed to stick in every Okinawan's craw.

Kedena was one of the main bases for Operation Arc Light which was, more or less, a continuation of Rolling Thunder. It was basically an attempt to end the war in Viet Nam by dropping a whole lot of bombs. Trying to combat guerrilla warfare with carpet bombing is a little like trying to wipe out a cockroach infestation with a sledge hammer. The enemy combatants or cockroaches you do manage to kill are as dead as dead can be but the process is terribly destructive and, in the end, not at all effective. We would wind up dropping more tons of bombs on Viet Nam than were dropped by both sides in all of WWII. In addition we dropped more bombs on Laos and Cambodia, two neutral countries, than we dropped on Hitler's Germany. It was going on for years before I came on the scene and went on after I left. Little if anything was accomplished.

It wasn't so much the B52 bombers that irked the locals it was the presence of nuclear weapons that played in the back of everybody's minds and would not let them rest. Although their existence was denied by authorities we all knew the A-bombs were there, hidden in caves somewhere near Kadena. If the war in Viet Nam escalated and China, 400 miles to the east, became involved or if the Chinese decided to take advantage of the situation to make a grab at Taiwan, 350 miles to the south, taking Okinawa off the board would be their first priority. It was the elephant in the room that we all wanted to ignore but couldn't.

In its wisdom the United States government saw to it that I had nothing to do with bombers or bombs. I was assigned to the Machinato Service Area as a welder. It soon became obvious that my welding skills did not measure up to any commercial standards. When I ran a bead it looked more like pigeon dropping on a ledge than a professional product. The top sergeant took me aside and asked if I welded at all before joining the army.

"Not one bit," I said in all honesty. "I was an art student at Pratt." I was reassigned as an illustrator/draftsman. This did not hurt my feeling one bit as Okinawa was a tropical Island and welding is hot work in any climate.

What the army did there at Machinato was to take busted trucks, jeeps and light armored vehicles for Viet Nam and completely refurbish them. The trucks and other damaged vehicles were delivered by ship and unloaded above the high water mark on the beach in front of the barracks. From there they were picked up by a giant forklift and driven up the hill to what amounted to a small automotive factory on the flat above the barracks. We were told that the large flat area, unusual for a coral island, was a former kamikaze landing strip from WWII. I thought to ask why kamikazes would need a landing strip but then thought better of it and didn't ask.

The broken vehicles went in one end of the factory where they were completely disassembled and then reassembled with new parts added as needed. When they rolled out the other end they looked like brand new, right down to the plastic on the seats.

Bob Hope and the USO came to Okinawa to put on a show. When he was touring the European Theater of Operations during WWII, with the Andrews Sisters and Dorsey Brothers, Bob was a patriotic hero and extremely relevant to the GIs he entertained. But 25 years later, when he arrived on The Rock, it was clear his time had passed.

We were told in advance that all non-essential personnel would be given the day off to attend the show. However, it soon became apparent that the majority of the unit planned to spend the day on the beach, the basketball court or in the bars of Nominui, the red light district of Naha City. Things weren't looking so good for Bob. It's true that Johnny Cash played Folsom Prison and it went over huge. But Johnny didn't spend his time before the show speaking the praises of wardens, prison guards and jails at every opportunity.

On the day of the show we were confined to barracks after morning formation and then, when the time came, we were marched to the makeshift amphitheater constructed for the event. Bob came out on stage and looked out over the crowd; out over the ever-widening generation gap. He was not fazed in the least but soldiered on winning over the audience. He also won my respect, at least for the man if not for his pro-war position.

When summer rolled around people on Okinawa started talking about typhoons. We were told that one hit the island in October of 1945 and sank more ships in a day than the kamikazes had managed to sink during the entire 12 weeks of the battle. The first typhoon alert came in July. I was a bit nervous as we taped off the windows of the concrete barracks and pushed our wall lockers into position to deflect flying glass.

As it turned out, typhoons were just an excuse for a party; an unexpected holiday like the school snow days of my youth. All the officers and higher ranking NCOs fled the base and we, the lowly conscripts, were left to fend for ourselves. Money was pooled and a last minute run was made to town for Akadama wine. This was not the cheap American wine we were used to drinking back in the states but the exotic cheap wine of the Orient. It came in a paper wrapper which featured a red circle. The choices were Akadama Red or Akadama White; they both tasted like each other and they both tasted more than a little like Thunderbird. For the most part they were used in conjunction with marijuana.

Our barracks, C Company, was one of a dozen on the slope of the hill just above the ocean. We could see the storm coming as it churned the sky over the East China Sea. It looked like a giant wheel of clouds or a spinning galaxy. The wind rose and so did the waves as they broke out over the coral flat.

I stood in front of the barracks and watched the typhoon approach from the east. The wind stiffened and the broken trucks that lined the beach began to sing as doors and windshields swung on hinges and canvas tops flapped. A fine mist hit my face and at first I took it for rain but when I licked it from my lips it tasted salty. From a thousand yards out to sea the tops of the waves were being blown off and were hitting against my face. It was time to go back in and join the party.

We sat around, played cards, drank wine and told stories. Just after noon the eye of the storm passed to the north of the island and the wind swung around coming hard and steady from the west. The back of the barracks was now feeling the full force while the front was in the lee. I don't know what made me think of it but I told the story of Robertson's ill-fated sheet/parachute jump from the balcony of the Medical Hold barracks back at Fort Dix. Paschal and Safford, two steadfast stoners from California, got it in their heads that the hypothesis was a sound one and the jump only failed because Robertson's execution was at fault. Between tokes of reefer and sips of wine they presented theories on how it could and should be done.

"A sheet just won't work. You need to use a blanket for something like that," Paschal observed.

"Yeah, man," Safford said

We had access to the roof of the two story building but I was determined to avoid a repeat of the unfortunate Medical Hold event. "Why don't you go out in front of the barracks in the relatively calm rotor of the wind and use that for a launching pad. Each one of you could take one end of the blanket and then dash around the corner and into the wind," I suggested.

"Wow," said Paschal. "That would be cool."

"Yeah, man" said Safford.

The vintage Korean War blanket held long enough to carry them four or five feet into the air and then ripped down the middle. They fell into a temporary pond formed by the driving rain and then tumbled down the hill towards B Company's barracks. The relentless wind thwarted their every attempt to get back up the hill.

This was not a problem as Paschal and Safford were likeable, good-natured dopers respected by all. They easily found a place in B Company's typhoon party. In fact, many from B Company had been watching the attempt at flight. Like Icarus and Daedalus the two were welcomed as the mythical characters they were.

PAY DAY

As I pointed out earlier, the United States Army of the late 1960s and early 70s was nothing like the Army we see today. The modern Army is all volunteers while we were, at least at the lower ranks, overwhelmingly conscripts -- guys who didn't want to be there at all. Today's Army accepts only highly motivated, high school graduates with clean police records. Back in the day we were a conglomeration of dopers, juicers, tramps, perpetrators, poppers, pot heads, acid heads, felons, certifiable morons, lushes, speed freaks, bag men, pimps, pushers, sociopaths, psychopaths, users, head cases, huffers, dealers, dream weavers, winos, goofballs, thieves and addicts of every kind.

On the island of Okinawa, drugs and alcohol were plentiful while supervision was minimal. No officers and very few enlisted men above the rank of E3 lived in the barracks. In the private rooms off the central hall were a few old sergeants who had been drinking and chain smoking since Guadalcanal. We called them lifers because they were on track to die in uniform, some sooner than others. We had little respect for them and, for the most part, they feared us. If they were in the barracks, and not at work or in a local bar, they locked themselves in their rooms with beverage of choice and hunkered down until morning.

The barracks itself had room for 150 soldiers but was never full. There was a mess hall on one end of the lower level and three large bays full of bunks; two up stairs and one down. The company was divided roughly into thirds. One third were people, like myself, who had some semblance of a job. Another third worked around the barracks. They cut grass, picked up trash, worked in the mess hall and handled general maintenance duties. The final third were troops under house arrest and awaiting trial for one transgression or another. This group kind of hung out all day. They had to be watched. We were one of a dozen companies that constituted the Machinado Service Area. Most of them were made up of the same components.

There was also a distinct black/white division within the company. This was about a 60/40 split in favor of white. Most of the blacks were the product of poor, inner city neighborhoods with picturesque names like Sandtown, Gardenia, Sweet Home, Cobb Creek and Buttermilk Bottom. Most of the whites came from impoverished rural towns with picturesque names like Sandtown, Gardenia, Sweet Home, Cobb Creek and Buttermilk Bottom.

With an eclectic mix of loosely supervised young men living in a confined space, problems are bound to arise. Throw in racial tensions along with virtually unlimited drugs and alcohol and it made for an extremely volatile situation. For the most part, the inmates were able to keep things under control during the week but weekends were always exciting and payday could be lethal.

Payday in the Army happened once a month and was considered a holiday. No one was expected to be at work. People spent pay day settling debts. The army supplied us with everything we needed to survive; food, clothing, shelter and a rudimentary sort of health care. The only things required by the Army, that we had to pay for out of our own pockets, were laundry service and haircuts. The three hundred or so dollars we received each month, on average, was more than enough to cover those expenses. But still, by the grace of one vice or another, much debt was incurred.

Troopers finding themselves short of funds at mid-month could always turn to Duce-and-a-half. He was built along the lines of the two and one-half ton truck which lent him his nickname and was always willing to help a fellow GI out at the tune of twenty percent interest. What Duce-and-a-half did was illegal so he was not allowed to collect in the dayroom where pay call was held but those who owed him money almost always sought him out and paid their debt. The few that Duce had to go and find served as an example for the rest that tardiness was not a virtue.

Duce-and-a-half was a professional loan shark having learned his craft in Detroit before being cornered by the Army. He never went beyond what was necessary to collect his money and if feathers had to be ruffled they were ruffled with measure and restraint. Most of the other violence associated with pay day lacked such grace. Given the fact that it was common knowledge throughout the island that on payday there would be thousands of servicemen walking around drunk or stoned or both and that they would all have money in their pockets it was not surprising that some of them were beaten and robbed every month. Payday was the most dangerous day of all.

Although Lieutenant Fletcher had no background in either trade, he was the officer in charge of our small group of draftsmen/illustrators. He had been working on his PhD in physics at an Ivy League university when his number came up in the draft. The Army made him an officer because of his advanced educational accomplishments, not for any flair he had for leadership. He got his nick-name, "The Fly," from the thick glasses he wore which magnified his eyes. The Fly was a thoroughly decent guy but, like many of us, completely out of his element in the military.

All officers had to take turns with payroll duty and, in due time, Lieutenant Fletcher's turn came. They told him he would need a guard but no MP was available to be assigned to him, he would have to pick his own. I was chosen for the task. We walked across base to the command offices and were given a canvas money bag containing the company payroll; about $35,000 dollars. They also gave us two big 45 caliber pistols in holsters with web belts; very John Wayne.

Now the urban black portion of our outfit all knew about guns from growing up on the streets. The rural whites all knew about guns from growing up in the woods. Perhaps the only two people in the company who didn't know squat about 45s were The Fly and myself. We did not know if they were loaded or even how we could tell if they were or not. I suggested there might be a button to push or something that had to be slid and began to fumble around with my gun. Lieutenant Fletcher, in his wisdom, took the gun away from me.

We made it to the end of the pay line without incident but on that last man we came up ten dollars short. There was extra money in the bag to make adjustments for such occurrences but we were expected to stay there after everybody left and go over the payroll again to see if we could find the error. We did and we didn't. It was now getting on towards sundown and if we did yet another recount we would be faced with the possibility of having to walk across base in the dark carrying a money bag.

Now you would think that two grown men would not be afraid to go out in the dark and that two soldiers armed with 45s would even welcome the experience. We did not. The Fly and I ponied up five dollars each and hightailed it across base before the sun set.

Two of the most important lessons I ever learned in my life I learned from Tooner. This is remarkable because I doubt he got much beyond the sixth grade and had an IQ somewhere around room temperature.

Tooner came into my life in 1970 while I was stationed at Machinato on Okinawa. I was hunched over my drawing board, reading the paper, when Lieutenant Fletcher stuck his head in the door and said to no one in particular. "I got a TDY in my office and I was wondering if you could find something for him to do for a few weeks." To say that The Fly did not like confrontation was an understatement; he did not even care much for conversation if it concerned subjects of a military nature. He made his announcement and was gone.

I was, more or less, in charge of the office. This was not because of my rank, which fluctuated too much for me to be anointed with any true symbol of power, but because nobody else was at all interested in the position. Darin was short, both in stature and in time remaining in the service. His body was on Okinawa but his head was already home in Cincinnati. Ortiz was from Puerto Rico. I hadn't known that people from Puerto Rico were susceptible to the draft but Ortiz was living proof that they were. His English wasn't very good and he had little interest in improving it. Mr. Hachimine, our local national, was wise enough to

know better than to assume any responsibility. It would only be a pain-in-the-ass and would, in the end, have no effect on his paycheck. We all knew The Fly's request was directed toward me. I went down the hall to pick up the TDY.

TDY was short for temporary duty. These were people assigned to an outfit for a matter of weeks or, at most, a few months. On the island of Okinawa they were usually GI's who had finished their year in Viet Nam but were still a few weeks away from their discharge date. Others had been wounded in action, treated and discharged from the Okinawa Army Hospital but were not yet ready to return to their units in the field. I'd seen TDYs around from time to time and even got to know a few but we never had one in our office before.

Tooner was small and wiry with that look of premature age that Viet Nam gave a man. He sat in the chair across from The Fly's desk. The man seemed placid enough except for the fingers on his left hand which drummed rhythmically on the arm of the chair. It was like watching the rocking of the relief valve on a pressure cooker.

The Fly was not there. He would not return until his office had been cleared of the TDY. "How long will you be with us?" I said as I sat down behind the desk.

Tooner didn't know the answer to that question and getting information from him in general proved to be quite difficult. It wasn't that he didn't want to talk; he just wasn't very good at it. I soon got the feeling that he wasn't any better at conversation than The Fly, he was just coming at it from the other end of the spectrum. It was, however, my job to find something for him to do while he was with us so I pressed on. I found out his first name was Cecil and that we could call him Cecil or Tooner. He didn't much care one way or the other. I could not see where one name had advantages over the other. I stuck with Tooner.

He had no physical limitations and hadn't been wounded. I got the feeling that he was there on Okinawa for some kind of stress related condition brought about by being too long in combat situations. These conditions were common among Okinawa TDYs.

"What did you do back in the world, you know, before you were in the army?" I asked in hope of gaining some insight.

"I sold balloons."

My curiosity was aroused. I guess that in my heart I always wanted to be a carny. I put my feet up on The Fly's desk, leaned back and asked the obvious followup questions. It seemed that Tooner traveled along behind small-time carnivals and county fairs and sold balloons out of his car in the parking lot. He wasn't affiliated with the show. Sometimes he was tolerated and sometime the proprietors of the carnival or fair tried to run him off. Tooner wasn't exactly a carny he was more like a carny wannabe. We were an office of draftsmen and illustrators. The matter of Tooner's civilian occupation was looking like a dead end.

"What did you do in Viet Nam?" I asked. I didn't think there would be much to work with here either. Previous experience with cutting out an LZ (landing zone) or fragging a hooch was of little use to us.

"I was a tunnel rat."

Tooner had me now. My feet came down on the floor and I sat up straight. Tunnel rats were the kind of thing that legends were made of.

The distance from Saigon, the capitol of South Viet Nam, to the Parrot's Beak, the Viet Cong staging area in Cambodia, was only about 30 miles. This stretch of jungle was visited by napalm, agent orange and B52s on Arc Light runs. It may well have been the most punished piece of real estate since the Romans salted Carthage. In time it become apparent that the entire distance was honeycombed with Viet Cong tunnels. The VC lived underground, virtually untouched, while the Americans rained down destruction from above.

American patrols were constantly on the hunt for the entrances to these tunnels and, when they found them, the tunnel rats came into play. These were men like Tooner; small, strong and utterly fearless. The rats, armed with only a flashlight and a 45 caliber pistol, would be sent in to clear the hole.

Sometimes the tunnels were abandoned and all that the rat could expect to find would be poisonous spiders, venomous snakes or booby traps of punji stakes and home-made hand grenades left behind by the previous tenants. Sometimes the tunnels were occupied and, if so, a whole platoon of Viet Cong could be lying in wait.

There were three tunnel rats in Tooner's unit and they took turns being the first one down into the hole. Tooner was spending time with us on Okinawa because he got in a fight with one of his fellow rats over who would have to go down a newly discovered hole.

211

"Isn't that just the Army way?" I said. "A man does something sane like refusing a suicide mission and they send him for psychological evaluation."

Tooner looked at me for quite a spell without speaking and then said, "It was his turn but I really wanted to go."

Now it was my opportunity to stand mute which I did flawlessly.

Tooner broke the silence, "What do you want me to do while I'm here?"

"Anything you want," I said.

What Tooner wanted to do was to sit outside in the shady alcove next to the soda machine and flip bottle caps in the direction of the trash can. He would hold the bottle caps between his thumb and middle finger and then snap his fingers sending the cap flying. After about two weeks of doing this for eight hours a day he became very proficient. He could curve them right or left, drop them straight down into the can or bank them off the wall. The soda machine provided an endless supply of caps.

This was the first lesson I learned from Tooner. Work at one thing long enough and hard enough and you will become good at it.

One morning, about four weeks into his sojourn, Tooner dropped a hospital form on my desk on his way to the soda machine alcove. The form said that he was ready to return to his outfit and all that was needed was an evaluation from his duty officer. The Fly, who was technically Tooners duty officer, had signed the form already. It was up to me to fill in the details.

I joined Tooner in the alcove and sat down in the next chair. "I don't know if there is anything I can do here but if you like I can fill out this form in such a manner as to confuse the issue. Maybe it can buy you another few week here on The Rock."

Tooner smiled at me. It was the first time I ever saw him smile. "I'm ready to go back," he said.

"How do you do it, how do you find the courage?" I asked.

"It doesn't scare me," he explained.

This was the second lesson I learned from Tooner. Courage isn't measured by the deed but by the amount of fear that has to be overcome in order to perform the deed.

"Just out of curiosity, what are you afraid of?" I asked.

"Women," was his reply.

MILITARY HISTORY EPILOGE

And then it all just ended. Two years earlier it had started as suddenly as Alice down the rabbit hole and then, just as suddenly, I was back on Tinker Street in Woodstock. But it wasn't the town I had left. The 1969 festival had transformed the place from a village with the mixed blessing of a summertime tourist season to a full-blown tourist town. The rhythms were different and I could never get in step. Trying my best to make the transition I lasted out the summer. But then, facing a Catskill Mountain winter, I packed my duffel bag one more time and headed south.

I never saw any of my Army friends again; not Big Red or One Lung, Butch, Salty Dog, The Fly or Tooner. There was no one even to nudge and say "Hey, remember the time…"

Made in the USA
Charleston, SC
19 May 2013